Five Stages of
GREEK RELIGION

FIVE STAGES OF GREEK RELIGION

BY

GILBERT MURRAY

Regius Professor of Greek
in the University of Oxford

GREENWOOD PRESS, PUBLISHERS
WESTPORT, CONNECTICUT

Library of Congress Cataloging in Publication Data

Murray, Gilbert, 1866-1957.
  Five stages of Greek religion.

  Reprint of the 1925 2d ed. published by Columbia
University Press, New York.
  Includes index.
  CONTENTS: Saturnia Regna.--The Olympian conquest.--
The great schools.--The failure of nerve.--The last pro-
test.--Appendix: Translation of the treatise of Sallust-
ius, Περὶ θεῶν καὶ κόσμου.
  1. Greece--Religion. I. Sallustius, Neoplatonius.
De diis et mundo. English. 1976. II. Title.
BL781.M8 1976   292'.1'3   76-27675
ISBN 0-8371-9080-0

This edition originally published in 1925 by Columbia University
Press, New York

This reprint has been authorized by the Clarendon Press Oxford

Reprinted in 1976 by Greenwood Press,
a division of Williamhouse-Regency Inc.

Library of Congress Catalog Card Number 76-27675

ISBN 0-8371-9080-0

Printed in the United States of America

PREFACE TO THE SECOND EDITION

In revising the *Four Stages of Greek Religion* I have found myself obliged to change its name. I felt there was a gap in the story. The high-water mark of Greek religious thought seems to me to have come just between the Olympian Religion and the Failure of Nerve; and the decline—if that is the right word—which is observable in the later ages of antiquity is a decline not from Olympianism but from the great spiritual and intellectual effort of the fourth century B. C., which culminated in the *Metaphysics* and the *De Anima* and the foundation of the Stoa and the Garden. Consequently I have added a new chapter at this point and raised the number of Stages to five.

My friend Mr. E. E. Genner has kindly enabled me to correct two or three errors in the first edition, and I owe special thanks to my old pupil, Professor E. R. Dodds, for several interesting observations and criticisms on points connected with Plotinus and Sallustius. Otherwise I have altered little. I am only sorry to have left the book so long out of print.

G. M.

PREFACE TO THE FIRST EDITION

THIS small book has taken a long time in growing. Though the first two essays were only put in writing this year for a course of lectures which I had the honour of delivering at Columbia University, the third, which was also used at Columbia, had in its main features appeared in the *Hibbert Journal* in 1910, the fourth in part in the *English Review* in 1908 ; the translation of Sallustius was made in 1907 for use with a small class at Oxford. Much of the material is much older in conception, and all has been reconsidered. I must thank the editors of both the above-named periodicals for their kind permission to reprint.

I think it was the writings of my friend Mr. Andrew Lang that first awoke me, in my undergraduate days, to the importance of anthropology and primitive religion to a Greek scholar. Certainly I began then to feel that the great works of the ancient Greek imagination are penetrated habitually by religious conceptions and postulates which literary scholars like myself had not observed or understood. In the meantime the situation has changed. Greek religion is being studied right and left, and has revealed itself as a surprisingly rich and attractive, though somewhat controversial, subject. It used to be a deserted territory; now it is at least a battle-ground. If ever the present differences resolved themselves into a simple fight with shillelaghs between the scholars and the anthropologists, I should without doubt wield my reluctant weapon on the side of the scholars. Scholarship is the rarer, harder, less popular and perhaps the more permanently valuable work, and it certainly stands more in need of defence at the moment. But in the meantime I can hardly understand how the purest of ' pure scholars ' can fail to feel his knowledge enriched by the savants who have compelled us to dig below the surface of our classical tradition and to realize the imaginative and historical problems which so often lie concealed beneath the smooth security of a verbal ' construe'. My own essays do not for a moment claim to speak with authority on a subject which is still changing and showing new facets year by year. They only claim to represent the way of regarding certain large issues of Greek Religion which has gradually taken shape, and has proved practically helpful and consistent with facts, in the mind of a very constant, though unsystematic, reader of many various periods of Greek literature.

In the first essay my debt to Miss Harrison is great and obvious. My statement of one or two points is

probably different from hers, but in the main I follow
her lead. And in either case I cannot adequately
describe the advantage I have derived from many years
of frequent discussion and comparison of results with
a Hellenist whose learning and originality of mind are
only equalled by her vivid generosity towards her
fellow-workers.

The second may also be said to have grown out of
Miss Harrison's writings. She has by now made the
title of ' Olympian ' almost a term of reproach, and
thrown down so many a scornful challenge to the
canonical gods of Greece, that I have ventured on
this attempt to explain their historical origin and plead
for their religious value. When the essay was already
written I read Mr. Chadwick's impressive book on
The Heroic Age (Cambridge, 1912), and was delighted
to find in an author whose standpoint and equipment
are so different from mine so much that confirmed or
clarified my own view.

The title of the third essay I owe to a conversation
with Professor J. B. Bury. We were discussing the
change that took place in Greek thought between,
say, Plato and the Neo-Platonists, or even between
Aristotle and Posidonius, and which is seen at its
highest power in the Gnostics. I had been calling it
a rise of asceticism, or mysticism, or religious passion,
or the like, when my friend corrected me. ' It is not

a rise ; it is a fall or failure of something, a sort of failure of nerve.'—We are treading here upon somewhat firmer ground than in the first two essays. The field for mere conjecture is less : we are supported more continuously by explicit documents. Yet the subject is a very difficult one owing to the scattered and chaotic nature of the sources, and even where we get away from fragments and reconstructions and reach definite treatises with or without authors' names, I cannot pretend to feel anything like the same clearness about the true meaning of a passage in Philo or the Corpus Hermeticum that one normally feels in a writer of the classical period. Consequently in this essay I think I have hugged my modern authorities rather close, and seldom expressed an opinion for which I could not find some fairly authoritative backing, my debt being particularly great to Reitzenstein, Bousset, and the brilliant *Hellenistisch-römische Kultur* of P. Wendland. I must also thank my old pupil, Mr. Edwyn Bevan, who was kind enough to read this book in proof, for some valuable criticisms. The subject is one of such extraordinary interest that I offer no apology for calling further attention to it.

A word or two about the last brief revival of the ancient religion under ' Julian the Apostate ' forms the natural close to this series of studies. But here our material, both historical and literary, is so abundant that I have followed a different method. After a short historical introduction I have translated in full a very curious and little-known ancient text, which may be said to constitute something like an authoritative Pagan creed. Some readers may regret that I do not give the Greek as well as the English. I am reluctant, however, to publish a text which I have not examined in the MSS., and I feel also that, while an edition of Sallustius is rather urgently needed, it ought to be an edition with a full commentary.

I was first led to these studies by the wish to fill up certain puzzling blanks of ignorance in my own mind, and doubtless the little book bears marks of this origin. It aims largely at the filling of interstices. It avoids the great illuminated places, and gives its mind to the stretches of intervening twilight. It deals little with the harvest of flowers or fruit, but watches the inconspicuous seasons when the soil is beginning to stir, the seeds are falling or ripening.

G. M.

CONTENTS

Ὁ πρῶτος ἄνθρωπος ἐκ γῆς, χοϊκός· ὁ δεύτερος ἄνθρωπος ὁ Κύριος ἐξ οὐρανοῦ.

'The first man is of the earth, earthy ; the second man is the Lord from heaven.'

I

SATURNIA REGNA

I

SATURNIA REGNA

Many persons who are quite prepared to admit the importance to the world of Greek poetry, Greek art, and Greek philosophy, may still feel it rather a paradox to be told that Greek religion specially repays our study at the present day. Greek religion, associated with a romantic, trivial, and not very edifying mythology, has generally seemed one of the weakest spots in the armour of those giants of the old world. Yet I will venture to make for Greek religion almost as great a claim as for the thought and the literature, not only because the whole mass of it is shot through by those strange lights of feeling and imagination, and the details of it constantly wrought into beauty by that instinctive sense of artistic form, which we specially associate with Classical Greece, but also for two definite historical reasons. In the first place, the student of that dark and fascinating department of the human mind which we may call Religious Origins, will find in Greece an extraordinary mass of material belonging to a very early date. For detail and variety the primitive Greek evidence has no equal. And, secondly, in this department as in others, ancient Greece has the triumphant if tragic distinction of beginning at the very bottom and struggling, however precariously, to the very summits. There is hardly

any horror of primitive superstition of which we cannot
find some distant traces in our Greek record. There
is hardly any height of spiritual thought attained in the
world that has not its archetype or its echo in the
stretch of Greek literature that lies between Thales and
Plotinus, embracing much of the ' Wisdom-Teachers '
and of St. Paul.

The progress of Greek religion falls naturally into
three stages, all of them historically important. First
there is the primitive *Euêtheia* or Age of Ignorance,
before Zeus came to trouble men's minds, a stage to
which our anthropologists and explorers have found
parallels in every part of the world. Dr. Preuss applies
to it the charming word ' Urdummheit ', or ' Primal
Stupidity '. In some ways characteristically Greek,
in others it is so typical of similar stages of thought
elsewhere that one is tempted to regard it as the
normal beginning of all religion, or almost as the
normal raw material out of which religion is made.
There is certainly some repulsiveness, but I confess
that to me there is also an element of fascination in
the study of these ' Beastly Devices of the Heathen ',
at any rate as they appear in early Greece, where each
single ' beastly device ' as it passes is somehow touched
with beauty and transformed by some spirit of upward
striving.

Secondly there is the Olympian or classical stage,
a stage in which, for good or ill, blunderingly or
successfully, this primitive vagueness was reduced to a
kind of order. This is the stage of the great Olympian gods, who dominated art and poetry, ruled the

imagination of Rome, and extended a kind of romantic dominion even over the Middle Ages. It is the stage that we learn, or mis-learn, from the statues and the handbooks of mythology. Critics have said that this Olympian stage has value only as art and not as religion. That is just one of the points into which we shall inquire.

Thirdly, there is the Hellenistic period, reaching roughly from Plato to St. Paul and the earlier Gnostics. The first edition of this book treated the whole period as one, but I have now divided it by writing a new chapter on the Movements of the Fourth Century B. C., and making that my third stage. This was the time when the Greek mind, still in its full creative vigour, made its first response to the twofold failure of the world in which it had put its faith, the open bankruptcy of the Olympian religion and the collapse of the city-state. Both had failed, and each tried vainly to supply the place of the other. Greece responded by the creation of two great permanent types of philosophy which have influenced human ethics ever since, the Cynic and Stoic schools on the one hand, and the Epicurean on the other. These schools belong properly, I think, to the history of religion. The successors of Aristotle produced rather a school of progressive science, those of Plato a school of refined scepticism. The religious side of Plato's thought was not revealed in its full power till the time of Plotinus in the third century A. D. ; that of Aristotle, one might say without undue paradox, not till its exposition by Aquinas in the thirteenth.

The old Third Stage, therefore, becomes now a Fourth, comprising the later and more popular movements of the Hellenistic Age, a period based on the consciousness of manifold failure, and consequently touched both with morbidity and with that spiritual exaltation which is so often the companion of morbidity. It not only had behind it the failure of the Olympian theology and of the free city-state, now crushed by semi-barbarous military monarchies; it lived through the gradual realization of two other failures—the failure of human government, even when backed by the power of Rome or the wealth of Egypt, to achieve a good life for man; and lastly the failure of the great propaganda of Hellenism, in which the long-drawn effort of Greece to educate a corrupt and barbaric world seemed only to lead to the corruption or barbarization of the very ideals which it sought to spread. This sense of failure, this progressive loss of hope in the world, in sober calculation, and in organized human effort, threw the later Greek back upon his own soul, upon the pursuit of personal holiness, upon emotions, mysteries and revelations, upon the comparative neglect of this transitory and imperfect world for the sake of some dream-world far off, which shall subsist without sin or corruption, the same yesterday, to-day, and for ever. These four are the really significant and formative periods of Greek religious thought; but we may well cast our eyes also on a fifth stage, not historically influential perhaps, but at least romantic and interesting and worthy of considerable respect, when the old religion in the time of Julian roused itself

for a last spiritual protest against the all-conquering
' atheism ' of the Christians. I omit Plotinus, as in
earlier chapters I have omitted Plato and Aristotle, and
for the same reason. As a rule in the writings of Julian's
circle and still more in the remains of popular belief,
the tendencies of our fourth stage are accentuated by
an increased demand for definite dogma and a still
deeper consciousness of worldly defeat.

I shall not start with any definition of religion.
Religion, like poetry and most other living things,
cannot be defined. But one may perhaps give some
description of it, or at least some characteristic marks.
In the first place, religion essentially deals with the
uncharted region of human experience. A large part
of human life has been thoroughly surveyed and
explored ; we understand the causes at work ; and we
are not bewildered by the problems. That is the
domain of positive knowledge. But all round us on
every side there is an uncharted region, just fragments
of the fringe of it explored, and those imperfectly ;
it is with this that religion deals. And secondly we
may note that religion deals with its own province not
tentatively, by the normal methods of patient intellectual research, but directly, and by methods of emotion
or sub-conscious apprehension. Agriculture, for instance, used to be entirely a question of religion ; now
it is almost entirely a question of science. In antiquity,
if a field was barren, the owner of it would probably
assume that the barrenness was due to ' pollution ', or
offence somewhere. He would run through all his own

possible offences, or at any rate those of his neighbours and ancestors, and when he eventually decided the cause of the trouble, the steps that he would take would all be of a kind calculated not to affect the chemical constitution of the soil, but to satisfy his own emotions of guilt and terror, or the imaginary emotions of the imaginary being he had offended. A modern man in the same predicament would probably not think of religion at all, at any rate in the earlier stages ; he would say it was a case for deeper ploughing or for basic slag. Later on, if disaster followed disaster till he began to feel himself a marked man, even the average modern would, I think, begin instinctively to reflect upon his sins. A third characteristic flows from the first. The uncharted region surrounds us on every side and is apparently infinite ; consequently, when once the things of the uncharted region are admitted as factors in our ordinary conduct of life they are apt to be infinite factors, overruling and swamping all others. The thing that religion forbids is a thing never to be done ; not all the inducements that this life can offer weigh at all in the balance. Indeed there is no balance. The man who makes terms with his conscience is essentially non-religious ; the religious man knows that it will profit him nothing if he gain all this finite world and lose his stake in the infinite and eternal.[1]

[1] Professor Émile Durkheim in his famous analysis of the religious emotions argues that when a man feels the belief and the command as something coming from without, superior, authoritative, of infinite import, it is because religion is the work of the tribe and, as such, superior to the individual. The voice of God is the imagined voice of

Am I going to draw no distinction then between religion and mere superstition? Not at present. Later on we may perhaps see some way to it. Superstition is the name given to a low or bad form of religion, to the kind of religion we disapprove. The line of division, if we made one, would be only an arbitrary bar thrust across a highly complex and continuous process.

Does this amount to an implication that all the religions that have existed in the world are false? Not so. It is obvious indeed that most, if analysed into intellectual beliefs, are false; and I suppose that

the whole tribe, heard or imagined by him who is going to break its laws. I have some difficulty about the psychology implied in this doctrine : surely the apparent externality of the religious command seems to belong to a fairly common type of experience, in which the personality is divided, so that first one part of it and then another emerges into consciousness. If you forget an engagement, sometimes your peace is disturbed for quite a long time by a vague external annoyance or condemnation, which at last grows to be a distinct judgement—'Heavens! I ought to be at the Committee on So-and-so.' But apart from this criticism, there is obviously much historical truth in Professor Durkheim's theory, and it is not so different as it seems at first sight from the ordinary beliefs of religious men. The tribe to primitive man is not a mere group of human beings. It is his whole world. The savage who is breaking the laws of his tribe has all his world—totems, tabus, earth, sky and all—against him. He cannot be at peace with God.

The position of the hero or martyr who defies his tribe for the sake of what he thinks the truth or the right can easily be thought out on these lines. He defies this false temporary Cosmos in loyalty to the true and permanent Cosmos.

See Durkheim, 'Les Formes élémentaires de la vie religieuse', in *Travaux de l'Année Sociologique*, 1912; or G. Davy, 'La Sociologie de M. Durkheim', in *Rev. Philosophique*, xxxvi, pp. 42-71 and 160-85.

a thoroughly orthodox member of any one of the
million religious bodies that exist in the world must be
clear in his mind that the other million minus one are
wrong, if not wickedly wrong. That, I think, we must
be clear about. Yet the fact remains that man must
have some relation towards the uncharted, the mys-
terious, tracts of life which surround him on every
side. And for my own part I am content to say that
his method must be to a large extent very much what
St. Paul calls πίστις or faith: that is, some attitude
not of the conscious intellect but of the whole being,
using all its powers of sensitiveness, all its feeblest and
most inarticulate feelers and tentacles, in the effort
somehow to touch by these that which cannot be
grasped by the definite senses or analysed by the
conscious reason. What we gain thus is an insecure
but a precious possession. We gain no dogma, at least
no safe dogma, but we gain much more. We gain
something hard to define, which lies at the heart not
only of religion, but of art and poetry and all the
higher strivings of human emotion. I believe that
at times we actually gain practical guidance in some
questions where experience and argument fail.[1] That

---

[1] I suspect that most reforms pass through this stage. A man
somehow feels clear that some new course is, for him, right, though
he cannot marshal the arguments convincingly in favour of it, and
may even admit that the weight of obvious evidence is on the other
side. We read of judges in the seventeenth century who believed
that witches ought to be burned and that the persons before them
were witches, and yet would not burn them—evidently under the
influence of vague half-realized feelings. I know a vegetarian who
thinks that, as far as he can see, carnivorous habits are not bad for

is a great work left for religion, but we must always remember two things about it : first, that the liability to error is enormous, indeed almost infinite ; and second, that the results of confident error are very terrible. Probably throughout history the worst things ever done in the world on a large scale by decent people have been done in the name of religion, and I do not think that has entirely ceased to be true at the present day. All the Middle Ages held the strange and, to our judgement, the obviously insane belief that the normal result of religious error was eternal punishment. And yet by the crimes to which that false belief led them they almost proved the truth of something very like it. The record of early Christian and medieval persecutions which were the direct result of that one confident religious error comes curiously near to one's conception of the wickedness of the damned.

To turn to our immediate subject, I wish to put forward here what is still a rather new and unauthorized view of the development of Greek religion ; readers will forgive me if, in treating so vast a subject, I draw my outline very broadly, leaving out many qualifications, and quoting only a fragment of the evidence.

human health and actually tend to increase the happiness of the species of animals eaten—as the adoption of Swift's *Modest Proposal* would doubtless relieve the economic troubles of the human race, and yet feels clear that for him the ordinary flesh meal (or ' feasting on corpses ') would ' partake of the nature of sin '. The path of progress is paved with inconsistencies, though it would be an error to imagine that the people who habitually reject any higher promptings that come to them are really any more consistent.

The things that have misled us moderns in our efforts towards understanding the primitive stage in Greek religion have been first the widespread and almost ineradicable error of treating Homer as primitive, and more generally our unconscious insistence on starting with the notion of ' Gods '. Mr. Hartland, in his address as president of one of the sections of the recent International Congress of Religions at Oxford,[1] dwelt on the significant fact about savage religions that wherever the word ' God ' is used our trustiest witnesses tend to contradict one another. Among the best observers of the Arunta tribes, for instance, some hold that they have no conception of God, others that they are constantly thinking about God. The truth is that this idea of a god far away in the sky—I do not say merely a First Cause who is ' without body parts or passions ', but almost any being that we should naturally call a ' god '—is an idea not easy for primitive man to grasp. It is a subtle and rarefied idea, saturated with ages of philosophy and speculation. And we must always remember that one of the chief religions of the world, Buddhism, has risen to great moral and intellectual heights without using the conception of God at all ; in his stead it has Dharma, the Eternal Law.[2]

Apart from some few philosophers, both Christian and Moslem, the gods of the ordinary man have as a rule been as a matter of course anthropomorphic. Men did not take the trouble to try to conceive them otherwise. In many cases they have had the

---

[1] *Transactions of the Third International Congress of Religions*, Oxford, 1908, pp. 26–7.   [2] *The Buddhist Dharma*, by Mrs. Rhys Davids.

actual bodily shape of man ; in almost all they have possessed—of course in their highest development— his mind and reason and his mental attributes. It causes most of us even now something of a shock to be told by a medieval Arab philosopher that to call God benevolent or righteous or to predicate of him any other human quality is just as Pagan and degraded as to say that he has a beard.[1] Now the Greek gods seem at first sight quite particularly solid and anthropomorphic. The statues and vases speak clearly, and they are mostly borne out by the literature. Of course we must discount the kind of evidence that misled Winckelmann, the mere Roman and Alexandrian art and mythology ; but even if we go back to the fifth century B. C. we shall find the ruling conceptions far nobler indeed, but still anthropomorphic. We find firmly established the Olympian patriarchal family, Zeus the Father of gods and men, his wife Hera, his son Apollo, his daughter Athena, his brothers Poseidon and Hades, and the rest. We probably think of each figure more or less as like a statue, a habit of mind obviously wrong and indeed absurd, as if one thought of ' Labour ' and ' Grief' as statues because Rodin or St. Gaudens has so represented them. And yet it was a habit into which the late Greeks themselves sometimes fell ;[2] their arts of sculpture and painting as applied to religion had been

---

[1] See *Die Mutaziliten, oder die Freidenker im Islam*, von H. Steiner, 1865. This Arab was clearly under the influence of Plotinus or some other Neo-Platonist.

[2] Cf. E. Reisch, *Entstehung und Wandel griechischer Göttergestalten*. Vienna, 1909.

so dangerously successful : they sharpened and made vivid an anthropomorphism which in its origin had been mostly the result of normal human laziness. The process of making winds and rivers into anthropomorphic gods is, for the most part, not the result of using the imagination with special vigour. It is the result of not doing so. The wind is obviously alive ; any fool can see that. Being alive, it blows ; how? why, naturally ; just as you and I blow. It knocks things down, it shouts and dances, it whispers and talks. And, unless we are going to make a great effort of the imagination and try to realize, like a scientific man, just what really happens, we naturally assume that it does these things in the normal way, in the only way we know. Even when you worship a beast or a stone, you practically anthropomorphize it. It happens indeed to have a perfectly clear shape, so you accept that. But it talks, acts, and fights just like a man—as you can see from the *Australian Folk Tales* published by Mrs. Langloh Parker—because you do not take the trouble to think out any other way of behaving. This kind of anthropomorphism—or as Mr. Gladstone used to call it, ' anthropophuism '—' humanity of *nature* '—is primitive and inevitable : the sharp-cut statue type of god is different, and is due in Greece directly to the work of the artists.

We must get back behind these gods of the artist's workshop and the romance-maker's imagination, and see if the religious thinkers of the great period use, or imply, the same highly human conceptions. We shall find Parmenides telling us that God coincides with the

universe, which is a sphere and immovable ;[1] Heraclitus, that God is 'day night, summer winter, war peace,
satiety hunger'. Xenophanes, that God is all-seeing, all-
hearing, and all mind ;[2] and as for his supposed human
shape, why, if bulls and lions were to speak about God
they would doubtless tell us that he was a bull or a lion.[3]
We must notice the instinctive language of the poets,
using the word θεός in many subtle senses for which
our word 'God' is too stiff, too personal, and too
anthropomorphic. Τὸ εὐτυχεῖν, 'the fact of success',
is 'a god and more than a god'; τὸ γιγνώσκειν φίλους,
'the thrill of recognizing a friend' after long absence,
is a 'god'; wine is a 'god' whose body is poured out
in libation to gods ; and in the unwritten law of the
human conscience 'a great god liveth and groweth not
old '.[4] You will say that is mere poetry or philosophy :
it represents a particular theory or a particular metaphor. I think not. Language of this sort is used widely
and without any explanation or apology. It was
evidently understood and felt to be natural by the

---

[1] Parm. Fr. 8, 3–7 (Diels²).
[2] Xen. Fr. 24 (Diels²).
[3] Xen. Fr. 15.
[4] Aesch. *Cho.* 60 ; Eur. *Hel.* 560 ; *Bac.* 284 ; Soph. *O.T.* 871.
Cf. also ἡ φρόνησις ἀγαθὴ θεὸς μέγας. Soph. Fr. 836, 2 (Nauck).

    ὁ πλοῦτος, ἀνθρωπίσκε, τοῖς σοφοῖς θεός. Eur. *Cycl.* 316.

    ὁ νοῦς γὰρ ἡμῶν ἐστιν ἐν ἑκάστῳ θεός. Eur. Fr. 1018.

    φθόνος κάκιστος κἀδικώτατος θεός. Hippothoön Fr. 2.

A certain moment of time : ἀρχὴ καὶ θεὸς ἐν ἀνθρώποις ἱδρυμένη σῴζει
πάντα. Pl. *Leg.* 775 E.

    τὰ μῶρα γὰρ πάντ' ἐστὶν 'Αφροδίτη βροτοῖς. Eur. *Tro.* 989.

    ἦλθεν δὲ δαὶς θάλεια πρεσβίστη θεῶν. Soph. Fr. 548.

audience. If it is metaphorical, all metaphors have grown from the soil of current thought and normal experience. And without going into the point at length I think we may safely conclude that the soil from which such language as this grew was not any system of clear-cut personal anthropomorphic theology. No doubt any of these poets, if he had to make a picture of one of these utterly formless Gods, would have given him a human form. That was the recognized symbol, as a veiled woman is St. Gaudens's symbol for ' Grief '.

But we have other evidence too which shows abundantly that these Olympian gods are not primary, but are imposed upon a background strangely unlike themselves. For a long time their luminous figures dazzled our eyes ; we were not able to see the half-lit regions behind them, the dark primeval tangle of desires and fears and dreams from which they drew their vitality. The surest test to apply in this question is the evidence of actual cult. Miss Harrison has here shown us the right method, and following her we will begin with the three great festivals of Athens, the Diasia, the Thesmophoria, and the Anthesteria.[1]

The Diasia was said to be the chief festival of Zeus, the central figure of the Olympians, though our authorities generally add an epithet to him, and call him Zeus Meilichios, Zeus of Placation. A god with an ' epithet ' is always suspicious, like a human

[1] See J. E. Harrison, *Prolegomena*, i, ii, iv ; Mommsen, *Feste der Stadt Athen*, 1898, pp. 308–22 (Thesmophoria), 384–404 (Anthesteria), 421–6 (Diasia). See also Pauly-Wissowa, s. v.

being with an ' alias '. Miss Harrison's examination (*Prolegomena*, pp. 28 ff.) shows that in the rites Zeus has no place at all. Meilichios from the beginning has a fairly secure one. On some of the reliefs Meilichios appears not as a god, but as an enormous bearded snake, a well-known representation of underworld powers or dead ancestors. Sometimes the great snake is alone ; sometimes he rises gigantic above the small human worshippers approaching him. And then, in certain reliefs, his old barbaric presence vanishes, and we have instead a benevolent and human father of gods and men, trying, as Miss Harrison somewhere expresses it, to look as if he had been there all the time.

There was a sacrifice at the Diasia, but it was not a sacrifice given to Zeus. To Zeus and all the heavenly gods men gave sacrifice in the form of a feast, in which the god had his portion and the worshippers theirs. The two parties cemented their friendship and feasted happily together. But the sacrifice at the Diasia was a holocaust : [1] every shred of the victim was burnt to ashes, that no man might partake of it. We know quite well the meaning of that form of sacrifice : it is a sacrifice to placate or appease the powers below, the Chthonioi, the dead and the lords of death. It was performed, as our authorities tell us, μετὰ στυγνό-τητος, with shuddering or repulsion.[2]

The Diasia was a ritual of placation, that is, of casting away various elements of pollution or danger and appeasing the unknown wraths of the surrounding

[1] *Prolegomena*, p. 15 f.
[2] Luc. *Icaro-Menippos* 24 schol. ad loc.

darkness. The nearest approach to a god contained in this festival is Meilichios, and Meilichios, as we shall see later, belongs to a particular class of shadowy beings who are built up out of ritual services. His name means ' *He of appeasement* ', and he is nothing else. He is merely the personified shadow or dream generated by the emotion of the ritual—very much, to take a familiar instance, as Father Christmas is a ' projection ' of our Christmas customs.

The Thesmophoria formed the great festival of Demeter and her daughter Korê, though here again Demeter appears with a clinging epithet, Thesmophoros. We know pretty clearly the whole course of the ritual : there is the carrying by women of certain magic charms, fir-cones and snakes and unnameable objects made of paste, to ensure fertility ; there is a sacrifice of pigs, who were thrown into a deep cleft of the earth, and their remains afterwards collected and scattered as a charm over the fields. There is more magic ritual, more carrying of sacred objects, a fast followed by a rejoicing, a disappearance of life below the earth, and a rising again of life above it ; but it is hard to find definite traces of any personal goddess. The Olympian Demeter and Persephone dwindle away as we look closer, and we are left with the shadow Thesmophoros, ' *She who carries Thesmoi* ',[1]

[1] Frequently dual, τὼ Θεσμοφόρω, under the influence of the ' Mother and Maiden ' idea : Dittenberger *Inscr. Sylloge* 628, Ar. *Thesm.* 84, 296 *et passim*. The plural αἱ Θεσμοφόροι used in late Greek is not, as one might imagine, a projection from the whole

not a substantive personal goddess, but merely a
personification of the ritual itself: an imaginary
Charm-bearer generated by so much charm-bearing,
just as Meilichios in the Diasia was generated from
the ritual of appeasement.

Now the Diasia were dominated by a sacred snake.
Is there any similar divine animal in the Thesmophoria?
Alas, yes. Both here, and still more markedly in the
mysteries of Demeter and Persephone at Eleusis, we
regularly find the most lovely of all goddesses, Demeter
and Persephone, habitually—I will not say represented
by, but dangerously associated with, a sacred Sow.
A Pig is the one animal in Greek religion that actually
had sacrifice made to it.[1]

The third feast, the Anthesteria, belongs in classical
times to the Olympian Dionysus, and is said to be the
oldest of his feasts. On the surface there is a touch of
the wine-god, and he is given due official prominence;
but as soon as we penetrate anywhere near the heart of
the festival, Dionysus and his brother gods are quite
forgotten, and all that remains is a great ritual for
appeasing the dead. All the days of the Feast were

band of worshippers; it is merely due to the disappearance of the
dual from Greek. I accept provisionally the derivation of these
θεσμοί from θεσ- in θέσσασθαι, θέσφατος, θέσκελος, πολύθεστος, ἀπό-
θεστος, &c.: cf. A. W. Verrall in *J. H. S.* xx, p. 114; and *Prolegomena*,
pp. 48 ff., 136 f. But, whatever the derivation, the Thesmoi were the
objects carried.

[1] Frazer, *Golden Bough*, ii. 44 ff.; A. B. Cook, *J. H. S.* xiv, pp. 153–
4; J. E. Harrison, *Themis*, p. 5. See also A. Lang, *Homeric Hymns*,
1899, p. 63.

nefasti, of ill omen ; the first day especially was ἐς τὸ
πᾶν ἀποφράς. On it the Wine Jars which were also
Seed and Funeral Jars were opened and the spirits of
the Dead let loose in the world.[1] Nameless and innumerable, the ghosts are summoned out of their
tombs, and are duly feasted, each man summoning his
own ghosts to his own house, and carefully abstaining
from any act that would affect his neighbours. And
then, when they are properly appeased and made
gentle, they are swept back again out of this world
to the place where they properly belong, and the
streets and houses cleaned from the presence of death.
There is one central stage indeed in which Dionysus
does seem to appear. And he appears in a very
significant way, to conduct a Sacred Marriage. For,
why do you suppose the dead are summoned at all?
What use to the tribe is the presence of all these
dead ancestors? They have come, I suspect, to be
born again, to begin a new life at the great Spring
festival. For the new births of the tribe, the new
crops, the new kids, the new human beings, are of
course really only the old ones returned to earth.[2]
The important thing is to get them properly placated
and purified, free from the contagion of ancient sin or
underworld anger. For nothing is so dangerous as the
presence of what I may call raw ghosts. The Anthesteria contained, like other feasts of the kind, a ἱερὸς

---

[1] *Feste der Stadt Athen*, p. 390 f. On Seed Jars, Wine Jars and
Funeral Jars, see *Themis*, pp. 276–88, and Warde Fowler, *Mundus
Patet*, in Journ. Roman Studies, ii, p. 25 ff. Cf. below, p. 43 f.

[2] Dieterich, *Muttererde*, 1905, p. 48 f.

γάμος, or Holy Marriage, between the wife of the Basileus or Sacred King, and the imaginary god.[1] Whatever reality there ever was in the ceremony has apparently by classical times faded away. But the place where the god received his bride is curious. It was called the Boukolion, or Bull's Shed. It was not originally the home of an anthropomorphic god, but of a divine animal.

Thus in each of these great festivals we find that the Olympian gods vanish away, and we are left with three things only: first, with an atmosphere of religious dread; second, with a whole sequence of magical ceremonies which, in two at least of the three cases,[2] produce

---

[1] Dr. Frazer, *The Magic Art*, ii. 137, thinks it not certain that the γάμος took place during the Anthesteria, at the same time as the oath of the γεραιραί. Without the γάμος, however, it is hard to see what the βασίλιννα and γεραιραί had to do in the festival; and this is the view of Mommsen, *Feste der Stadt Athen*, pp. 391–3; Gruppe in Iwan Müller, *Mythologie und Religionsgeschichte*, i. 33; Farnell, *Cults*, v. 217.

[2] One might perhaps say, in all three. Ἀνθίστηρος τοῦ Πυθοχρηστοῦ κοινόν is the name of a society of worshippers in the island of Thera, *I. G. I.* iii. 329. This gives a god Anthister, who is clearly identified with Dionysus, and seems to be a projection of a feast Anthisteria = Anthesteria. The inscription is of the second century B. C. and it seems likely that Anthister–Anthisteria, with their clear derivation from ἀνθίζειν, are corruptions of the earlier and difficult forms Ἀνθέστηρ– Ἀνθεστήρια. It is noteworthy that Thera, an island lying rather outside the main channels of civilization, kept up throughout its history a tendency to treat the 'epithet' as a full person. Hikesios and Koures come very early; also Polieus and Stoichaios without the name Zeus; Delphinios, Karneios, Aiglatas, and Aguieus without Apollo. See Hiller von Gaertringen in the *Festschrift für O. Benndorff*, p. 228. Also Nilsson, *Griechische Feste*, 1906, p. 267, n. 5.

a kind of strange personal emanation of themselves, the Appeasements producing Meilichios, the Charm-bearings Thesmophoros ; and thirdly, with a divine or sacred animal. In the Diasia we find the old super-human snake, who reappears so ubiquitously throughout Greece, the regular symbol of the underworld powers, especially the hero or dead ancestor. Why the snake was so chosen we can only surmise. He obviously lived underground : his home was among the Chthonioi, the Earth-People. Also, says the Scholiast to Aristophanes (*Plut.* 533), he was a type of new birth because he throws off his old skin and renews himself. And if that in itself is not enough to show his supernatural power, what normal earthly being could send his enemies to death by one little pin-prick, as some snakes can?

In the Thesmophoria we found sacred swine, and the reason given by the ancients is no doubt the right one. The sow is sacred because of its fertility, and possibly as practical people we should add, because of its cheapness. Swine are always prominent in Greek agricul-tural rites. And the bull? Well, we modern town-dwellers have almost forgotten what a real bull is like. For so many centuries we have tamed him and penned him in, and utterly deposed him from his place as lord of the forest. The bull was the chief of magic or sacred animals in Greece, chief because of his enormous strength, his size, his rage, in fine, as anthropologists call it, his *mana*; that primitive word which comprises force, vitality, prestige, holiness, and power of magic, and which may belong equally to a lion, a chief, a medicine-man, or a battle-axe.

Now in the art and the handbooks these sacred animals have all been adopted into the Olympian system. They appear regularly as the ' attributes ' of particular gods. Zeus is merely accompanied by a snake, an eagle, a bull, or at worst assumes for his private purposes the forms of those animals. The cow and the cuckoo are sacred to Hera ; the owl and the snake to Athena ; the dolphin, the crow, the lizard, the bull, to Apollo. Dionysus, always like a wilder and less middle-aged Zeus, appears freely as a snake, bull, he-goat, and lion. Allowing for some isolated exceptions, the safest rule in all these cases is that the attribute is original and the god is added.[1] It comes out very clearly in the case of the snake and the bull. The tremendous *mana* of the wild bull indeed occupies almost half the stage of pre-Olympian ritual. The religion unearthed by Dr. Evans in Crete is permeated by the bull of Minos. The heads and horns are in almost every sacred room and on every altar. The great religious scene depicted on the sarcophagus of Hagia Triada [2] centres in the holy blood that flows from the neck of a captive and dying bull. Down into classical times bull's blood was a sacred thing which it was dangerous to touch and death to taste : to drink a cup of it was the most heroic

---

[1] Miss Harrison, ' Bird and Pillar Worship in relation to Ouranian Divinities ', *Transactions of the Third International Congress for the History of Religion*, Oxford, 1908, vol. ii, p. 154 ; Farnell, *Greece and Babylon*, 1911, pp. 66 ff.

[2] First published by R. Paribeni, ' Il Sarcofago dipinto di Hagia Triada ', in *Monumenti antichi della R. Accademia dei Lincei*, xix, 1908, p. 6, T. i–iii. See also *Themis*, pp. 158 ff.

form of suicide.[1] The sacrificial bull at Delphi was called *Hosiôtêr* : he was not merely *hosios*, holy ; he was *Hosiôtêr*, the Sanctifier, He who maketh Holy. It was by contact with him that holiness was spread to others. On a coin and a vase, cited by Miss Harrison,[2] we have a bull entering a holy cave and a bull standing in a shrine. We have holy pillars whose holiness consists in the fact that they have been touched with the blood of a bull. We have a long record of a bull-ritual at Magnesia,[3] in which Zeus, though he makes a kind of external claim to be lord of the feast, dare not claim that the bull is sacrificed to him. Zeus has a ram to himself and stands apart, showing but a weak and shadowy figure beside the original Holy One. We have immense masses of evidence about the religion of Mithras, at one time the most serious rival of Christianity, which sought its hope and its salvation in the blood of a divine bull.

Now what is the origin of this conception of the sacred animal ? It was first discovered and explained with almost prophetic insight by Dr. Robertson Smith.[4] The origin is what he calls a sacramental feast : you eat the flesh and drink the blood of the divine animal in order—here I diverge from Robertson Smith's language—to get into you his *mana*, his vital power. The classical instance is the sacramental

---

[1] Ar. *Equites*, 82-4—or possibly of apotheosis. See *Themis*, p. 154, n. 2.　　　　[2] *Themis*, p. 145, fig. 25 ; and p. 152, fig. 28 b.

[3] O. Kern, *Inschriften v. Magnesia*, No. 98, discussed by O. Kern, *Arch. Anz.* 1894, p. 78, and Nilsson, *Griechische Feste*, p. 23.

[4] *Religion of the Semites*, 1901, p. 338 ; Reuterskiold, in *Archiv f. Relig.* xv. 1-23.

eating of a camel by an Arab tribe, recorded in the works of St. Nilus.[1] The camel was devoured on a particular day at the rising of the morning star. He was cut to pieces alive, and every fragment of him had to be consumed before the sun rose. If the life had once gone out of the flesh and blood the sacrifice would have been spoilt ; it was the spirit, the vitality, of the camel that his tribesmen wanted. The only serious error that later students have found in Robertson Smith's statement is that he spoke too definitely of the sacrifice as affording communion with the tribal god. There was no god there, only the raw material out of which gods are made. You devoured the holy animal to get its *mana*, its swiftness, its strength, its great endurance, just as the savage now will eat his enemy's brain or heart or hands to get some particular quality residing there. The imagination of the pre-Hellenic tribes was evidently dominated above all things by the bull, though there were other sacramental feasts too, combined with sundry horrible rendings and drinkings of raw blood. It is strange to think that even small things like kids and fawns and hares should have struck primitive man as having some uncanny vitality which he longed for, or at least some uncanny power over the weather or the crops. Yet to him it no doubt appeared obvious. Frogs, for instance, could always bring rain by croaking for it, and who can limit the powers and the knowledge of birds ? [2]

[1] *Nili Opera, Narrat.* iii. 28.

[2] See Aristophanes' *Birds*, e. g. 685–736 : cf. the practice of augury from birds, and the art-types of Winged Kêres, Victories and Angels.

Here comes a difficulty. If the Olympian god was
not there to start with, how did he originate ? We can
understand—at least after a course of anthropology—
this desire of primitive man to acquire for himself the
superhuman forces of the bull ; but how does he make
the transition from the real animal to the imaginary
human god ? First let us remember the innate tendency of primitive man everywhere, and not especially
in Greece, to imagine a personal cause, like himself in
all points not otherwise specified, for every striking
phenomenon. If the wind blows it is because some
being more or less human, though of course super-
human, is blowing with his cheeks. If a tree is struck
by lightning it is because some one has thrown his
battle-axe at it. In some Australian tribes there is no
belief in natural death. If a man dies it is because
' bad man kill that fellow '. St. Paul, we may remember, passionately summoned the heathen to refrain
from worshipping τὴν κτίσιν, the creation, and go back
to τὸν κτίσαντα, the creator, human and masculine. It
was as a rule a road that they were only too ready
to travel.[1]

But this tendency was helped by a second factor.
Research has shown us the existence in early Mediterranean religion of a peculiar transitional step, a man
wearing the head or skin of a holy beast. The
Egyptian gods are depicted as men with beasts' heads :
that is, the best authorities tell us, their shapes are
derived from the kings and priests who on great
occasions of sacrifice covered their heads with a beast-

[1] Romans, i. 25 ; viii. 20–3.

mask.[1] Minos, with his projection the Minotaur, was
a bull-god and wore a bull-mask. From early Island
gems, from a fresco at Mycenae, from Assyrian reliefs,
Mr. A. B. Cook has collected many examples of this
mixed figure—a man wearing the *protomê*, or mask and
mane, of a beast. Sometimes we can actually see him
offering libations. Sometimes the worshipper has
become so closely identified with his divine beast
that he is represented not as a mere man wearing the
protomê of a lion or bull, but actually as a lion or bull
wearing the *protomê* of another.[2] Hera, βοῶπις, with
a cow's head; Athena, γλαυκῶπις, with an owl's head,
or bearing on her breast the head of the Gorgon;
Heracles clad in a lion's skin and covering his brow δεινῷ
χάσματι θηρός, 'with the awful spread jaws of the wild
beast', belong to the same class. So does the Dadouchos
at Eleusis and other initiators who let candidates for
purification set one foot—one only and that the left—
on the skin of a sacrificial ram, and called the skin Διὸς
κῷας, the fleece not of a ram, but of Zeus.[3]

The *mana* of the slain beast is in the hide and head
and blood and fur, and the man who wants to be in
thorough contact with the divinity gets inside the skin

---

[1] Lang, *Myth, Ritual, and Religion*, 1906, ii. 284; ibid., 130; Moret,
Caractère religieux de la Monarchie Égyptienne; Dieterich, *Mithrasliturgie*, 1903.

[2] A. B. Cook in *J. H. S.* 1894, 'Animal Worship in the Mycenaean
Age'. See also Hogarth on the 'Zakro Sealings', *J. H. S.* 1902; these
seals show a riot of fancy in the way of mixed monsters, starting in all
probability from the simpler form. See the quotation from Robertson
Smith in Hogarth, p. 91.

[3] *Feste der Stadt Athen*, p. 416.

and wraps himself deep in it. He begins by being
a man wearing a lion's skin : he ends, as we have seen,
by feeling himself to be a lion wearing a lion's skin.
And who is this man ? He may on particular occasions
be only a candidate for purification or initiation. But
par excellence he who has the right is the priest, the
medicine-man, the divine king. If an old suggestion
of my own is right, he is the original θεός or θεσός, the
incarnate medicine or spell or magic power.[1] He at
first, I suspect, is the only θεός or 'God' that his
society knows. We commonly speak of ancient kings
being 'deified'; we regard the process as due to an
outburst of superstition or insane flattery. And so no
doubt it sometimes was, especially in later times—when
man and god were felt as two utterly distinct things.
But 'deification' is an unintelligent and misleading
word. What we call 'deification' is only the survival
of this undifferentiated human θεός, with his *mana*, his
κράτος and βία, his control of the weather, the rain and
the thunder, the spring crops and the autumn floods ;
his knowledge of what was lawful and what was not, and
his innate power to curse or to 'make dead'. Recent
researchers have shown us in abundance the early
Greek medicine-chiefs making thunder and lightning
and rain.[2] We have long known the king as possessor
of Dike and Themis, of justice and tribal custom ; we
have known his effect on the fertility of the fields and

---

[1] *Anthropology and the Classics*, 1908, pp. 77, 78.

[2] A. B. Cook, *Class. Rev.* xvii, pp. 275 ff. ; A. J. Reinach, *Rev. de
l'Hist. des Religions*, lx, p. 178 ; S. Reinach, *Cultes, Mythes, &c.*, ii.
160–6.

the tribes, and the terrible results of a king's sin or a king's sickness.[1]

What is the subsequent history of this medicine-chief or θεός? He is differentiated, as it were: the visible part of him becomes merely human; the supposed supernatural part grows into what we should call a God. The process is simple. Any particular medicine-man is bound to have his failures. As Dr. Frazer gently reminds us, every single pretension which he puts forth on every day of his life is a lie, and liable sooner or later to be found out. Doubtless men are tender to their own delusions. They do not at once condemn the medicine-chief as a fraudulent institution, but they tend gradually to say that he is not the real all-powerful θεός. He is only his representative. The real θεός, tremendous, infallible, is somewhere far away, hidden in clouds perhaps, on the summit of some inaccessible mountain. If the mountain is once climbed the god will move to the upper sky. The medicine-chief meanwhile stays on earth, still influential. He has some connexion with the great god more intimate than that of other men; at worst he possesses the god's sacred instruments, his ἱερά or ὄργια; he knows the rules for approaching him and making prayers to him.

There is therefore a path open from the divine beast to the anthropomorphic god. From beings like

[1] One may suggest in passing that this explains the enormous families attributed to many sacred kings of Greek legend: why Priam or Danaus have their fifty children, and Heracles, most prolific of all, his several hundred. The particular numbers chosen, however, are probably due to other causes, e. g. the fifty moon-months of the Penteteris.

Thesmophoros and Meilichios the road is of course much easier. They are already more than half anthropomorphic; they only lack the concreteness, the lucid shape and the detailed personal history of the Olympians. In this connexion we must not forget the power of hallucination, still fairly strong, as the history of religious revivals in America will bear witness,[1] but far stronger, of course, among the impressionable hordes of early men. 'The god', says M. Doutté in his profound study of Algerian magic, 'c'est le désir collectif personnifié', the collective desire projected, as it were, or personified.[2] Think of the gods who have appeared in great crises of battle, created sometimes by the desperate desire of men who have for years prayed to them, and who are now at the last extremity for lack of their aid, sometimes by the confused and excited remembrances of the survivors after the victory. The gods who led the Roman charge at Lake Regillus,[3] the gigantic figures that were seen fighting before the Greeks at Marathon,[4] even the celestial signs that promised Constantine victory for the cross:[5]—these are the effects of great emotion: we can all understand them. But even in daily life primitive men seem to have dealt more freely than we generally do with apparitions

[1] See *Primitive Traits in Religious Revivals*, by F. M. Davenport. New York, 1906.

[2] E. Doutté, *Magie et religion dans l'Afrique du Nord*, 1909, p. 601.

[3] Cicero, *de Nat. Deorum*, ii. 2 ; iii. 5, 6 ; Florus, ii. 12.

[4] Plut. *Theseus*, 35 ; Paus. i. 32. 5. Herodotus only mentions a bearded and gigantic figure who struck Epizelos blind (vi. 117).

[5] Eusebius, *Vit. Constant.*, l. i, cc. 28, 29, 30 ; *Nazarius inter Panegyr. Vet.* x. 14, 15.

and voices and daemons of every kind. One of the most
remarkable and noteworthy sources for this kind of
hallucinatory god in early societies is a social custom
that we have almost forgotten, the religious Dance.
When the initiated young men of Crete or elsewhere
danced at night over the mountains in the Oreibasia or
Mountain Walk they not only did things that seemed
beyond their ordinary workaday strength; they also felt
themselves led on and on by some power which guided
and sustained them. This daemon has no necessary
name : a man may be named after him ' Oreibasius ',
' Belonging to the Mountain Dancer ', just as others
may be named ' Apollonius ' or ' Dionysius '. The god
is only the spirit of the Mountain Dance, Oreibates,
though of course he is absorbed at different times in
various Olympians. There is one god called Aphiktor,
the Suppliant, He who prays for mercy. He is just
the projection, as M. Doutté would say, of the intense
emotion of one of those strange processions well known
in the ancient world, bands of despairing men or women
who have thrown away all means of self-defence and
join together at some holy place in one passionate
prayer for pity. The highest of all gods, Zeus, was
the special patron of the suppliant ; and it is strange
and instructive to find that Zeus the all-powerful
is actually identified with this Aphiktor : Ζεὺς μὲν
Ἀφίκτωρ ἐπίδοι προφρόνως.[1] The assembled prayer,
the united cry that rises from the oppressed of the

---

[1] Aesch. *Suppl.* 1, cf. 478 Ζεὺς ἱκτήρ. *Rise of the Greek Epic*[3],
p. 275 n. Adjectival phrases like Ζεὺς Ἱκέσιος, Ἱκετήσιος, Ἱκταῖος are
common and call for no remark.

world, is itself grown to be a god, and the greatest god. A similar projection arose from the dance of the *Kouroi*, or initiate youths, in the dithyramb—the magic dance which was to celebrate, or more properly, to hasten and strengthen, the coming on of spring. That dance projected the Megistos Kouros, the greatest of youths, who is the incarnation of spring or the return of life, and lies at the back of so many of the most gracious shapes of the classical pantheon. The Kouros appears as Dionysus, as Apollo, as Hermes, as Ares : in our clearest and most detailed piece of evidence he actually appears with the characteristic history and attributes of Zeus.[1]

This spirit of the dance, who leads it or personifies its emotion, stands more clearly perhaps than any other daemon half-way between earth and heaven. A number of difficult passages in Euripides' *Bacchae* and other Dionysiac literature find their explanations when we realize how the god is in part merely identified with the inspired chief dancer, in part he is the intangible projected incarnation of the emotion of the dance.

' The collective desire personified ' : on what does the collective desire, or collective dread, of the primitive community chiefly concentrate ? On two things, the food-supply and the tribe-supply, the desire not to die of famine and not to be harried or conquered by the neighbouring tribe. The fertility of the earth and the fertility of the tribe, these two are felt in early religion

---

[1] Hymn of the Kouretes, *Themis*, passim.

as one.[1] The earth is a mother : the human mother
is an ἄρουρα, or ploughed field. This earth-mother is
the characteristic and central feature of the early
Aegean religions. The introduction of agriculture
made her a mother of fruits and corn, and it is in that
form that we best know her. But in earlier days she
had been a mother of the spontaneous growth of the
soil, of wild beasts and trees and all the life of the
mountain.[2] In early Crete she stands with lions erect
on either side of her or with snakes held in her hands
and coiled about her body. And as the earth is mother
when the harvest comes, so in spring she is maiden
or Korê, but a maiden fated each year to be wedded
and made fruitful ; and earlier still there has been the
terrible time when fields are bare and lifeless. The
Korê has been snatched away underground, among the
dead peoples, and men must wait expectant till the
first buds begin to show and they call her to rise again
with the flowers. Meantime earth as she brings
forth vegetation in spring is Kourotrophos, rearer of
Kouroi, or the young men of the tribe. The nymphs
and rivers are all Kourotrophoi. The Moon is
Kourotrophos. She quickens the young of the tribe

[1] See in general I. King, *The Development of Religion*, 1910 ; E. J.
Payne, *History of the New World*, 1892, p. 414. Also Dieterich,
Muttererde, esp. pp. 37–58.

[2] See Dieterich, *Muttererde*, J. E. Harrison, *Prolegomena*, chap. vi,
' The Making of a Goddess ' ; *Themis*, chap. vi, ' The Spring Drômenon '. As to the prehistoric art-type of this goddess technically called
' steatopygous ', I cannot refrain from suggesting that it may be
derived from a mountain Δ turned into a human figure, as the palladion
or figure-8 type came from two round shields. See p. 73.

in their mother's womb ; at one terrible hour especially she is ' a lion to women ' who have offended against her holiness. ✓She also marks the seasons of sowing and ploughing, and the due time for the ripening of crops. When men learn to calculate in longer units, the Sun appears : they turn to the Sun for their calendar, and at all times of course the Sun has been a power in agriculture. He is not called Kourotrophos, but the Young Sun returning after winter is himself a Kouros,[1] and all the Kouroi have some touch of the Sun in them. The Cretan Spring-song of the Kouretes prays for νέοι πολῖται, young citizens, quite simply among the other gifts of the spring.[2]

This is best shown by the rites of tribal initiation, which seem normally to have formed part of the spring Drômena or sacred performances. The Kouroi, as we have said, are the initiated young men. They pass through their initiation; they become no longer παῖδες, boys, but ἄνδρες, men. The actual name Kouros is possibly connected with κείρειν, to shave,[3] and may mean that after this ceremony they first cut their long hair.

[1] *Hymn Orph.* 8, 10 ὡροτρόφε κοῦρε.

[2] For the order in which men generally proceed in worship, turning their attention to (1) the momentary incidents of weather, rain, sunshine, thunder, &c. ; (2) the Moon ; (3) the Sun and stars, see Payne, *History of the New World called America*, vol. i, p. 474, cited by Miss Harrison, *Themis*, p. 390.

[3] On the subject of Initiations see Webster, *Primitive Secret Societies*, New York, 1908 ; Schurtz, *Altersklassen und Männerbunde*, Berlin, 1902 ; Van Gennep, *Rites de Passage*, Paris, 1909 ; Nilsson, *Grundlage des Spartanischen Lebens* in Klio xii (1912), pp. 308–40 ; *Themis*, p. 337, n. 1. Since the above, Rivers, *Social Organization*, 1924.

Till then the κοῦρος is ἀκερσεκόμης—with hair un-shorn. They have now open to them the two roads that belong to ἄνδρες alone : they have the work of begetting children for the tribe, and the work of killing the tribe's enemies in battle.

The classification of people according to their age is apt to be sharp and vivid in primitive communities. We, for example, think of an old man as a kind of man and an old woman as a kind of woman ; but in primitive peoples as soon as a man and woman cease to be able to perform his and her due tribal functions they cease to be men and women, ἄνδρες and γυναῖκες : the ex-man becomes a γέρων ; the ex-woman a γραῦς.[1] We distinguish between 'boy' and 'man', between 'girl' and 'woman' ; but apart from the various words for baby, Attic Greek would have four sharp divisions, παῖς, ἔφηβος, ἀνήρ, γέρων.[2] In Sparta the divisions are still sharper and more numerous, cen-tring in the great initiation ceremonies of the Iranes, or full-grown youths, to the goddess called Orthia or Bortheia.[3] These initiation ceremonies are called

---

[1] Cf. Dr. Rivers on *mate*, 'Primitive Conception of Death', *Hibbert Journal*, January 1912, p. 393.

[2] Cf. Cardinal Virtues, Pindar, *Nem*. iii. 72 :

> ἐν παισὶ νέοισι παῖς, ἐν ἀνδράσιν ἀνήρ, τρίτον
> ἐν παλαιτέροισι μέρος, ἕκαστον οἷον ἔχομεν
> βρότεον ἔθνος. ἐλᾷ δὲ καὶ τέσσαρας ἀρετὰς
> ὁ θνατὸς αἰών,

also Pindar, *Pyth*. iv. 281.

[3] See Woodward in *B. S. A.* xiv, 83. Nikagoras won four (suc-cessive ?) victories as μικκιχιζόμενος, πρόπαις, παῖς, and μελλείρην, i. e. from his tenth to fifteenth year. He would then at 14 or 15 become

Teletai, 'completions': they mark the great 'rite of transition' from the immature, charming, but half useless thing which we call boy or girl, to the τέλειος ἀνήρ, the full member of the tribe as fighter or counsellor, or to the τελεία γυνή, the full wife and mother. This whole subject of Greek initiation ceremonies calls pressingly for more investigation. It is only in the last few years that we have obtained the material for understanding them, and the whole mass of the evidence needs re-treatment. For one instance, it is clear that a great number of rites which were formerly explained as remnants of human sacrifice are simply ceremonies of initiation.[1]

At the great spring Drômenon the tribe and the growing earth were renovated together: the earth arises afresh from her dead seeds, the tribe from its dead ancestors; and the whole process, charged as it is with the emotion of pressing human desire, projects its anthropomorphic god or daemon. A vegetation-spirit we call him, very inadequately; he is a divine Kouros, a Year-Daemon, a spirit that in the first stage is living, then dies with each year, then thirdly rises again from the dead, raising the whole dead world with him—the Greeks called him in this phase 'the Third One', or the 'Saviour'. The renovation ceremonies were accom-

an *iran*. Plut. *Lyc.* 17 gives the age of an *iran* as 20. This agrees with the age of an ἔφηβος at Athens as '15-20', '14-21', 'about 16'; see authorities in Stephanus s. v. ἔφηβος. Such variations in the date of 'puberty ceremonies' are common.

[1] See *Rise of the Greek Epic*, Appendix on Hym. Dem.; and W. R. Halliday, *C. R.* xxv, 8. Nilsson's valuable article has appeared since the above was written (see note 3, p. 46).

panied by a casting off of the old year, the old garments, and everything that is polluted by the infection of death. And not only of death ; but clearly I think, in spite of the protests of some Hellenists, of guilt or sin also. For the life of the Year-Daemon, as it seems to be reflected in Tragedy, is generally a story of Pride and Punishment. Each Year arrives, waxes great, commits the sin of Hubris, and then is slain. The death is deserved ; but the slaying is a sin : hence comes the next Year as Avenger, or as the Wronged One re-risen. 'All things pay retribution for their injustice one to another according to the ordinance of time.'[1] It is this range of ideas, half suppressed during the classical period, but evidently still current among the ruder and less Hellenized peoples, which supplied St. Paul with some of his most famous and deep-reaching metaphors. 'Thou fool, that which thou sowest is not quickened except it die.'[2] 'As He was raised from the dead we may walk with Him in newness of life.' And this renovation must be preceded by a casting out and killing of the old polluted life—' the old man in us must first be crucified '.

'The old man must be crucified.' We observed that in all the three Festivals there was a pervasive element of vague fear. Hitherto we have been dealing

[1] Anaximander apud Simplic. phys. 24, 13 ; Diels, *Fragmente der Vorsokratiker*, i. 13. See especially F. M. Cornford, *From Religion to Philosophy* (Cambridge, 1912), i ; also my article on English and Greek Tragedy in *Essays of the Oxford English School*, 1912. This explanation of the τρίτος σωτήρ is my conjecture.

[2] 1 Cor. xv. 36 ; Rom. vi generally, 3–11.

with early Greek religion chiefly from the point of view
of *mana*, the positive power or force that man tries to
acquire from his totem-animal or his god.   But there
is also a negative side to be considered : there is not
only the *mana*, but the *tabu*, the Forbidden, the Thing
Feared. We must cast away the old year ; we must
put our sins on to a φαρμακός or scapegoat and drive it
out. When the ghosts have returned and feasted with
us at the Anthesteria we must, with tar and branches of
buckthorn, purge them out of every corner of the rooms
till the air is pure from the infection of death. We must
avoid speaking dangerous words ; in great moments
we must avoid speaking any words at all, lest there
should be even in the most innocent of them some
unknown danger ; for we are surrounded above and
below by Kêres, or Spirits, winged influences, shapeless or of unknown shape, sometimes the spirits of death,
sometimes of disease, madness, calamity ; thousands
and thousands of them, as Sarpedon says, from whom
man can never escape nor hide ;[1] 'all the air so
crowded with them', says an unknown ancient poet,
'that there is not one empty chink into which you
could push the spike of a blade of corn.'[2]

The extraordinary security of our modern life in
times of peace makes it hard for us to realize, except
by a definite effort of the imagination, the constant
precariousness, the frightful proximity of death, that

---

[1] *Il.* M. 326 f. μυρίαι, ἃς οὐκ ἔστι φυγεῖν βροτὸν οὐδ᾽ ὑπαλύξαι.

[2] Frg. Ap. Plut. *Consol. ad Apoll.* xxvi ... ὅτι " πλείη μὲν γαῖα κακῶν
πλείη δὲ θάλασσα " καὶ " τοιάδε θνητοῖσι κακὰ κακῶν ἀμφί τε κῆρες
εἰλεῦνται, κενεὴ δ᾽ εἴσδυσις οὐδ᾽ ἀθέρι " (MS. αἰθέρι).

was usual in these weak ancient communities. They were in fear of wild beasts ; they were helpless against floods, helpless against pestilences. Their food depended on the crops of one tiny plot of ground ; and if the Saviour was not reborn with the spring, they slowly and miserably died. And all the while they knew almost nothing of the real causes that made crops succeed or fail. They only felt sure it was somehow a matter of pollution, of unexpiated defilement. It is this state of things that explains the curious cruelty of early agricultural doings, the human sacrifices, the scapegoats, the tearing in pieces of living animals, and perhaps of living men, the steeping of the fields in blood. Like most cruelty it has its roots in terror, terror of the breach of *Tabu*—the Forbidden Thing. I will not dwell on this side of the picture : it is well enough known. But we have to remember that, like so many morbid growths of the human mind, it has its sublime side. We must not forget that the human victims were often volunteers. The records of Carthage and Jerusalem, the long list in Greek legend of princes and princesses who died for their country, tell the same story. In most human societies, savage as well as civilized, it is not hard to find men who are ready to endure death for their fellow-citizens. We need not suppose that the martyrs were always the noblest of the human race. They were sometimes mad—hysterical or megalomaniac : sometimes reckless and desperate : sometimes, as in the curious case attested of the Roman armies on the Danube, they were men of strong desires and weak imagination ready to die at the end of a short period, if in the meantime they might glut all their senses with unlimited indulgence.[1]

Still, when all is said, there is nothing that stirs men's imagination like the contemplation of martyrdom, and it is no wonder that the more emotional cults of antiquity vibrate with the worship of this dying Saviour, the Sôsipolis, the Sôtêr, who in so many forms dies with his world or for his world, and rises again as the world rises, triumphant through suffering over Death and the broken *Tabu*.

Tabu is at first sight a far more prominent element in the primitive religions than *Mana*, just as misfortune and crime are more highly coloured and striking than prosperity and decent behaviour. To an early Greek tribe the world of possible action was sharply divided between what was Themis and what was Not Themis, between lawful and *tabu*, holy and unholy, correct and forbidden. To do a thing that was not Themis was a sure source of public disaster. Consequently it was of the first necessity in a life full of such perils to find out the exact rules about them. How is that to be managed ? Themis is ancient law : it is τὰ πάτρια, the way of our ancestors, the thing that has always been done and is therefore divinely right. In ordinary life, of course, Themis is clear. Every one knows it.

---

[1] Frazer, *Lectures on the Early History of the Kingship*, 267 ; F. Cumont, 'Les Actes de S. Dasius', in *Analecta Bollandiana*, xvi. 5–16 ; cf. especially what St. Augustine says about the disreputable hordes of would-be martyrs called *Circumcelliones*. See Index to Augustine, vol. xi in Migne : some passages collected in Seeck, *Gesch. d. Untergangs der antiken Welt*, vol. iii, Anhang, pp. 503 ff.

But from time to time new emergencies arise, the like of which we have never seen, and they frighten us. We must go to the Gerontes, the Old Men of the Tribe ; they will perhaps remember what our fathers did. What they tell us will be *Presbiston*, a word which means indifferently 'oldest' and 'best'—αἰεὶ δὲ νεώτεροι ἀφραδέουσιν, 'Young men are always being foolish '. Of course, if there is a Basileus, a holy King, he by his special power may perhaps know best of all, though he too must take care not to gainsay the Old Men.

For the whole problem is to find out τὰ πάτρια, the ways that our fathers followed. And suppose the Old Men themselves fail us, what must we needs do ? Here we come to a famous and peculiar Greek custom, for which I have never seen quoted any exact parallel or any satisfactory explanation. If the Old Men fail us, we must go to those older still, go to our great ancestors, the ἥρωες, the Chthonian people, lying in their sacred tombs, and ask them to help. The word χρᾶν means both ' to lend money ' and ' to give an oracle ', two ways of helping people in an emergency. Sometimes a tribe might happen to have a real ancestor buried in the neighbourhood ; if so, his tomb would be an oracle. More often perhaps, for the memories of savage tribes are very precarious, there would be no well-recorded personal tomb. The oracle would be at some place sacred to the Chthonian people in general, or to some particular personification of them, a Delphi or a cave of Trophônius, a place of Snakes and Earth. You go to the Chthonian folk for guidance because they are themselves the Oldest of the Old Ones, and they

know the real custom : they know what is Presbiston,
what is Themis. And by an easy extension of this
knowledge they are also supposed to know what is.
He who knows the law fully to the uttermost also
knows what will happen if the law is broken. It is,
I think, important to realize that the normal reason
for consulting an oracle was not to ask questions of
fact. It was that some emergency had arisen in which
men simply wanted to know how they ought to behave.
The advice they received in this way varied from
the virtuous to the abominable, as the religion itself
varied. A great mass of oracles can be quoted enjoining
the rules of customary morality, justice, honesty, piety,
duty to a man's parents, to the old, and to the weak.
But of necessity the oracles hated change and strangled
the progress of knowledge. Also, like most manifestations of early religion, they throve upon human terror :
the more blind the terror the stronger became their
hold. In such an atmosphere the lowest and most
beastlike elements of humanity tended to come to
the front ; and religion no doubt as a rule joined with
them in drowning the voice of criticism and of civilization, that is, of reason and of mercy. When really
frightened the oracle generally fell back on some remedy
full of pain and blood. The medieval plan of burning
heretics alive had not yet been invented. But the
history of uncivilized man, if it were written, would
provide a vast list of victims, all of them innocent, who
died or suffered to expiate some portent or *monstrum*—
some reported τέρας—with which they had nothing
whatever to do, which was in no way altered by their

suffering, which probably never really happened at all, and if it did was of no consequence. The sins of the modern world in dealing with heretics and witches have perhaps been more gigantic than those of primitive men, but one can hardly rise from the record of these ancient observances without being haunted by the judgement of the Roman poet :

Tantum religio potuit suadere malorum,

and feeling with him that the lightening of this cloud, the taming of this blind dragon, must rank among the very greatest services that Hellenism wrought for mankind.

II

THE OLYMPIAN CONQUEST

II

THE OLYMPIAN CONQUEST

I. *Origin of the Olympians*

THE historian of early Greece must find himself often on the watch for a particular cardinal moment, generally impossible to date in time and sometimes hard even to define in terms of development, when the clear outline that we call Classical Greece begins to take shape out of the mist. It is the moment when, as Herodotus puts it, ' the Hellenic race was marked off from the barbarian, as more intelligent and more emancipated from silly nonsense '.[1] In the eighth century B. C., for instance, so far as our remains indicate, there cannot have been much to show that the inhabitants of Attica and Boeotia and the Peloponnese were markedly superior to those of, say, Lycia or Phrygia, or even Epirus. By the middle of the fifth century the difference is enormous. On the one side is Hellas, on the other the motley tribes of ' barbaroi '.

When the change does come and is consciously felt

---

[1] Hdt. i. 60 ἐπεί γε ἀπεκρίθη ἐκ παλαιτέρου τοῦ βαρβάρου ἔθνεος τὸ Ἑλληνικὸν ἐὸν καὶ δεξιώτερον καὶ εὐηθίης ἠλιθίου ἀπηλλαγμένον μᾶλλον. As to the date here suggested for the definite dawn of Hellenism Mr. Edwyn Bevan writes to me : ' I have often wondered what the reason is that about that time a new age began all over the world that we know. In Nearer Asia the old Semitic monarchies gave place to the Zoroastrian Aryans; in India it was the time of Buddha, in China of Confucius.' Εὐηθίη ἠλίθιος is almost ' *Urdummheit* '.

we may notice a significant fact about it. It does not announce itself as what it was, a new thing in the world. It professes to be a revival, or rather an emphatic realization, of something very old. The new spirit of classical Greece, with all its humanity, its intellectual life, its genius for poetry and art, describes itself merely as being ' Hellenic '—like the Hellenes. And the Hellenes were simply, as far as we can make out, much the same as the Achaioi, one of the many tribes of predatory Northmen who had swept down on the Aegean kingdoms in the dawn of Greek history.[1]

This claim of a new thing to be old is, in varying degrees, a common characteristic of great movements. The Reformation professed to be a return to the Bible, the Evangelical movement in England a return to the Gospels, the High Church movement a return to the early Church. A large element even in the French Revolution, the greatest of all breaches with the past, had for its ideal a return to Roman republican virtue or to the simplicity of the natural man.[2] I noticed quite lately a speech of an American Progressive leader claiming that his principles were simply those of Abraham Lincoln. The tendency is due in part to the almost insuperable difficulty of really inventing a new

[1] See in general Ridgeway, *Early Age of Greece*, vol. i ; Leaf, *Companion to Homer*, Introduction ; *R. G. E.*, chap. ii ; Chadwick, *The Heroic Age* (last four chapters) ; and J. L. Myres, *Dawn of History*, chaps. viii and ix.

[2] Since writing the above I find in Vandal, *L'Avènement de Bonaparte*, p. 20, in Nelson's edition, a phrase about the Revolutionary soldiers : ' Ils se modelaient sur ces Romains . . . sur ces Spartiates . . . et ils créaient un type de haute vertu guerrière, quand ils croyaient seulement le reproduire.'

word to denote a new thing. It is so much easier to take an existing word, especially a famous word with fine associations, and twist it into a new sense. In part, no doubt, it comes from mankind's natural love for these old associations, and the fact that nearly all people who are worth much have in them some instinctive spirit of reverence. Even when striking out a new path they like to feel that they are following at least the spirit of one greater than themselves.

The Hellenism of the sixth and fifth centuries was to a great extent what the Hellenism of later ages was almost entirely, an ideal and a standard of culture. The classical Greeks were not, strictly speaking, pure Hellenes by blood. Herodotus and Thucydides [1] are quite clear about that. The original Hellenes were a particular conquering tribe of great prestige, which attracted the surrounding tribes to follow it, imitate it, and call themselves by its name. The Spartans were, to Herodotus, Hellenic ; the Athenians on the other hand were not. They were Pelasgian, but by a certain time ' changed into Hellenes and learnt the language '. In historical times we cannot really find any tribe of pure Hellenes in existence, though the name clings faintly to a particular district, not otherwise important, in South Thessaly. Had there been any undoubted Hellenes with incontrovertible pedigrees still going, very likely the ideal would have taken quite a different name. But where no one's ancestry would bear much inspection, the only way to show you were a true Hellene was to behave as such : that is, to approximate

---

[1] Hdt. i. 56 f. ; Th. i. 3 (Hellen son of Deucalion, in both).

to some constantly rising ideal of what the true Hellene should be. In all probability if a Greek of the fifth century, like Aeschylus or even Pindar, had met a group of the real Hellenes or Achaioi of the Migrations, he would have set them down as so many obvious and flaming barbarians.

We do not know whether the old Hellenes had any general word to denote the surrounding peoples ('Pelasgians and divers other barbarous tribes' [1]) whom they conquered or accepted as allies.[2] In any case by the time of the Persian Wars (say 500 B. C.) all these tribes together considered themselves Hellenized, bore the name of ' Hellenes ', and formed a kind of unity against hordes of ' barbaroi ' surrounding them on every side and threatening them especially from the east.

Let us consider for a moment the dates. In political history this self-realization of the Greek tribes as Hellenes against barbarians seems to have been first felt in the Ionian settlements on the coast of Asia Minor, where the ' sons of Javan ' (Yawan = Ἰάων) clashed as invaders against the native Hittite and Semite. It was emphasized by a similar clash in the further colonies in Pontus and in the West. If we wish for a central moment as representing this self-realization of Greece, I should be inclined to find it

---

[1] Hdt. i. 58. In viii. 44 the account is more detailed.

[2] The Homeric evidence is, as usual, inconclusive. The word βάρβαροι is absent from both poems, an absence which must be intentional on the part of the later reciters, but may well come from the original sources. The compound βαρβαρόφωνοι occurs in B 867, but who knows the date of that particular line in that particular wording ?

in the reign of Pisistratus (560–527 B. C.) when that monarch made, as it were, the first sketch of an Athenian empire based on alliances and took over to Athens the leadership of the Ionian race.

In literature the decisive moment is clear. It came when, in Mr. Mackail's phrase, ' Homer came to Hellas '.[1] The date is apparently the same, and the influences at work are the same. It seems to have been under Pisistratus that the Homeric Poems, in some form or other, came from Ionia to be recited in a fixed order at the Panathenaic Festival, and to find a canonical form and a central home in Athens till the end of the classical period. Athens is the centre from which Homeric influence radiates over the mainland of Greece. Its effect upon literature was of course enormous. It can be traced in various ways. By the content of the literature, which now begins to be filled with the heroic saga. By a change of style which emerges in, say, Pindar and Aeschylus when compared with what we know of Corinna or Thespis. More objectively and definitely it can be traced in a remarkable change of dialect. The old Attic poets, like Solon, were comparatively little affected by the epic influence ; the later elegists, like Ion, Euenus, and Plato, were steeped in it.[2]

---

[1] Paper read to the Classical Association at Birmingham in 1908.

[2] For Korinna see Wilamowitz in *Berliner Klassikertexte*, V. xiv, especially p. 55. The Homeric epos drove out poetry like Corinna's. She had actually written : ' I sing the great deeds of heroes and heroines ' (ἰώνει δ' εἰρώων ἀρετὰς χειρωιάδων ἀίδω, fr. 10, Bergk), so that presumably her style was sufficiently ' heroic ' for an un-Homeric generation. For the change of dialect in elegy, &c., see Thumb

In religion the cardinal moment is the same. It consists in the coming of Homer's ' Olympian Gods ', and that is to be the subject of the present essay. I am not, of course, going to describe the cults and characters of the various Olympians. For that inquiry the reader will naturally go to the five learned volumes of my colleague, Dr. Farnell. I wish merely to face certain difficult and, I think, hitherto unsolved problems affecting the meaning and origin and history of the Olympians as a whole.

Herodotus in a famous passage tells us that Homer and Hesiod ' made the generations of the Gods for the Greeks and gave them their names and distinguished their offices and crafts and portrayed their shapes ' (2. 53). The date of this wholesale proceeding was, he thinks, perhaps as much as four hundred years before his own day (*c.* 430 B. C.) but not more. Before that time the Pelasgians—i. e. the primitive inhabitants of Greece as opposed to the Hellenes— were worshipping gods in indefinite numbers, with no particular names ; many of them appear as figures carved emblematically with sex-emblems to represent the powers of fertility and generation, like the Athenian ' Herms '. The whole account bristles with points for discussion, but in general it suits very well with the picture drawn in the first of these essays, with its Earth Maidens and Mothers and its projected Kouroi.

Handbuch d. gr. Dialekte, pp. 327–30, 368 ff., and the literature there cited. Fick and Hoffmann overstated the change, but Hoffmann's new statement in *Die griechische Sprache*, 1911, sections on *Die Elegie*, seems just. The question of Tyrtaeus is complicated by other problems.

The background is the pre-Hellenic 'Urdummheit';
the new shape impressed upon it is the great anthropomorphic Olympian family, as defined in the Homeric
epos and, more timidly, in Hesiod. But of Hesiod
we must speak later.

Now who are these Olympian Gods and where do
they come from? Homer did not 'make' them out
of nothing. But the understanding of them is beset
with problems.

In the first place why are they called 'Olympian'?
Are they the Gods of Mount Olympus, the old sacred
mountain of Homer's Achaioi, or do they belong to
the great sanctuary of Olympia in which Zeus, the lord
of the Olympians, had his greatest festival? The two
are at opposite ends of Greece, Olympus in North
Thessaly in the north-east, Olympia in Elis in the
south-west. From which do the Olympians come?
On the one hand it is clear in Homer that they dwell
on Mount Olympus; they have 'Olympian houses'
beyond human sight, on the top of the sacred mountain, which in the Odyssey is identified with heaven.
On the other hand, when Pisistratus introduced the
worship of Olympian Zeus on a great scale into Athens
and built the Olympieum, he seems to have brought
him straight from Olympia in Elis. For he introduced
the special Elean complex of gods, Zeus, Rhea, Kronos,
and Gê Olympia.[1]

Fortunately this puzzle can be solved. The Olym-

---

[1] The facts are well known : see Paus. i. 18. 7. The inference was
pointed out to me by Miss Harrison.

pians belong to both places. It is merely a case of tribal migration. History, confirmed by the study of the Greek dialects, seems to show that these northern Achaioi came down across central Greece and the Gulf of Corinth and settled in Elis.[1] They brought with them their Zeus, who was already called 'Olympian', and established him as superior to the existing god, Kronos. The Games became Olympian and the sanctuary by which they were performed 'Olympia'.[2]

As soon as this point is clear, we understand also why there is more than one Mount Olympus. We can all think of two, one in Thessaly and one across the Aegean in Mysia. But there are many more; some twenty-odd, if I mistake not, in the whole Greek region. It is a pre-Greek word applied to mountains; and it seems clear that the 'Olympian' gods, wherever their worshippers moved, tended to dwell in the highest mountain in the neighbourhood, and the mountain thereby became Olympus.

The name, then, explains itself. The Olympians are the mountain gods of the old invading Northmen, the chieftains and princes, each with his *comitatus* or loose following of retainers and minor chieftains, who

---

[1] I do not here raise the question how far the Achaioi have special affinities with the north-west group of tribes or dialects. See Thumb, *Handbuch d. gr. Dialekte* (1909), p. 166 f. The Achaioi must have passed through South Thessaly in any case.

[2] That Kronos was in possession of the Kronion and Olympia generally before Zeus came was recognized in antiquity; Paus. v. 7. 4 and 10. Also Mayer in Roscher's Lexicon, ii, p. 1508, 50 ff.; *Rise of Greek Epic*,[3] pp. 40–8; J. A. K. Thomson. *Studies in the Odyssey* (1914), chap. vii, viii; Chadwick, *Heroic Age* (1911), pp. 282, 289.

broke in upon the ordered splendours of the Aegean palaces and, still more important, on the ordered simplicity of tribal life in the pre-Hellenic villages of the mainland. Now, it is a canon of religious study that all gods reflect the social state, past or present, of their worshippers. From this point of view what appearance do the Olympians of Homer make? What are they there for? What do they do, and what are their relations one to another?

The gods of most nations claim to have created the world. The Olympians make no such claim. The most they ever did was to conquer it. Zeus and his *comitatus* conquered Cronos and his; conquered and expelled them—sent them migrating beyond the horizon, Heaven knows where. Zeus took the chief dominion and remained a permanent overlord, but he apportioned large kingdoms to his brothers Hades and Poseidon, and confirmed various of his children and followers in lesser fiefs. Apollo went off on his own adventure and conquered Delphi. Athena conquered the Giants. She gained Athens by a conquest over Poseidon, a point of which we will speak later.

And when they have conquered their kingdoms, what do they do? Do they attend to the government? Do they promote agriculture? Do they practise trades and industries? Not a bit of it. Why should they do any honest work? They find it easier to live on the revenues and blast with thunderbolts the people who do not pay. They are conquering chieftains, royal buccaneers. They fight, and feast, and play, and make music; they drink deep, and roar with laughter at the lame smith who waits on them. They are never afraid, except of their own king. They never tell lies, except in love and war.

A few deductions may be made from this statement, but they do not affect its main significance. One god, you may say, Hephaistos, is definitely a craftsman. Yes: a smith, a maker of weapons. The one craftsman that a gang of warriors needed to have by them; and they preferred him lame, so that he should not run away. Again, Apollo herded for hire the cattle of Admetus; Apollo and Poseidon built the walls of Troy for Laomedon. Certainly in such stories we have an intrusion of other elements; but in any case the work done is not habitual work, it is a special punishment. Again, it is not denied that the Olympians have some effect on agriculture and on justice: they destroy the harvests of those who offend them, they punish oath-breakers and the like. Even in the Heroic Age itself—if we may adopt Mr. Chadwick's convenient title for the Age of the Migrations—chieftains and gods probably retained some vestiges of the functions they had exercised in more normal and settled times; and besides we must always realize that, in these inquiries, we never meet a simple and uniform figure. We must further remember that these gods are not real people with a real character. They never existed. They are only concepts, exceedingly confused cloudy and changing concepts, in the minds of thousands of diverse worshippers and non-worshippers. They change every time they are thought of, as a word changes every time it is pronounced. Even in the height of the Achaean wars the concept of any one god would be mixed up with traditions and associations drawn from the surrounding populations and their gods ; and by the time they come down to us in Homer and our other early literature, they have passed through the minds of many different ages and places, especially Ionia and Athens.

The Olympians as described in our text of Homer, or as described in the Athenian recitations of the sixth century, are *mutatis mutandis* related to the Olympians of the Heroic Age much as the Hellenes of the sixth century are to the Hellenes of the Heroic Age. I say ' *mutatis mutandis* ', because the historical development of a group of imaginary concepts shrined in tradition and romance can never be quite the same as that of the people who conceive them. The realm of fiction is apt both to leap in front and to lag in the rear of the march of real life. Romance will hug picturesque darknesses as well as invent perfections. But the gods of Homer, as we have them, certainly seem to show traces of the process through which they have passed : of an origin among the old conquering Achaioi, a development in the Ionian epic schools, and a final home in Athens.[1]

---

[1] I do not touch here on the subject of the gradual expurgation of the Poems to suit the feelings of a more civilized audience ; see *Rise of the Greek Epic*,[3] pp. 120-4. Many scholars believe that the Poems did not exist as a written book till the public copy was made by Pisistratus ; see Cauer, *Grundfragen der Homerkritik* [2] (1909), pp. 113-45 ; *R. G. E.*,[3] pp. 304-16 ; Leaf, *Iliad*, vol. i, p. xvi. This view is tempting, though the evidence seems to be insufficient to justify a pronouncement either way. If it is true, then various passages which show a verbal use of earlier documents (like the Bellerophon

For example, what gods are chiefly prominent in Homer? In the *Iliad* certainly three, Zeus, Apollo, and Athena, and much the same would hold for the *Odyssey*. Next to them in importance will be Poseidon, Hera, and Hermes.

Zeus stands somewhat apart. He is one of the very few gods with recognizable and undoubted Indo-germanic names, Djēus, the well-attested sky- and rain-god of the Aryan race. He is Achaian; he is ' Hellanios ', the god worshipped by all Hellenes. He is also, curiously enough, Pelasgian, and Mr. A. B. Cook [1] can explain to us the seeming contradiction. But the Northern elements in the conception of Zeus have on the whole triumphed over any Pelasgian or Aegean sky-god with which they may have mingled, and Zeus, in spite of his dark hair, may be mainly treated as the patriarchal god of the invading Northmen, passing from the Upper Danube down by his three great sanctuaries, Dodona, Olympus, and Olympia. He had an extraordinary power of ousting or absorbing the various objects of aboriginal worship which he found in his path. The story of Meilichios above (p. 28) is a common one. Of course, we must not suppose that the Zeus of the actual Achaioi was a figure quite like the Zeus of Pheidias or of Homer. There has been a good deal of expurgation in the Homeric Zeus,[2] as

passage, *R. G. E.*,[3] pp. 175 ff.) cannot have been put in before the Athenian period.

[1] In his *Zeus, the Indo-European Sky-God* (1914, 1924). See *R. G. E.*,[3] pp. 40 ff.

[2] A somewhat similar change occurred in Othin, though he always retains more of the crooked wizard.

Mr. Cook clearly shows. The Counsellor and Cloud-compeller of classical Athens was the wizard and rain-maker of earlier times ; and the All-Father surprises us in Thera and Crete by appearing both as a babe and as a Kouros in spring dances and initiation rituals.[1] It is a long way from these conceptions to the Zeus of Aeschylus, a figure as sublime as the Jehovah of Job ; but the lineage seems clear.

Zeus is the Achaean Sky-god. His son Phoebus Apollo is of more complex make. On one side he is clearly a Northman. He has connexions with the Hyperboreans.[2] He has a ' sacred road ' leading far into the North, along which offerings are sent back from shrine to shrine beyond the bounds of Greek knowledge. Such ' sacred roads ' are normally the roads by which the God himself has travelled ; the offerings are sent back from the new sanctuary to the old. On the other side Apollo reaches back to an Aegean matriarchal Kouros. His home is Delos, where he has a mother, Leto, but no very visible father. He leads the ships of his islanders, sometimes in the form of a dolphin. He is no ' Hellene '. In the fighting at Troy he is against the Achaioi : he destroys the Greek host, he champions Hector, he even slays Achilles. In the Homeric hymn to Apollo we read that when the great archer draws near to Olympus all the gods tremble and start from their seats ; Leto alone, and of course Zeus, hold their ground.[3] What

---

[1] *Themis*, chap. i. On the Zeus of Aeschylus cf. *R. G. E.*,[3] pp. 277 ff. ; Gomperz, *Greek Thinkers*, ii. 6–8.

[2] Farnell, *Cults*, iv. 100–4. See, however, Gruppe, p. 107 f.

[3] *Hymn. Ap.* init. Cf. Wilamowitz's Oxford Lecture on ' Apollo ' (Oxford, 1907).

this god's original name was at Delos we cannot be sure : he has very many names and 'epithets'. But he early became identified with a similar god at Delphi and adopted his name, 'Apollôn', or, in the Delphic and Dorian form, 'Apellôn'—presumably the Kouros projected from the Dorian gatherings called 'apellae'.[1] As Phoibos he is a sun-god, and from classical times onward we often find him definitely identified with the Sun, a distinction which came easily to a Kouros.

In any case, and this is the important point, he is at Delos the chief god of the Ionians. The Ionians are defined by Herodotus as those tribes and cities who were sprung from Athens and kept the Apaturia. They recognized Delos as their holy place and worshipped Apollo Patrôos as their ancestor.[2] The Ionian Homer has naturally brought us the Ionian god ; and, significantly enough, though the tradition makes him an enemy of the Greeks, and the poets have to accept the tradition, there is no tendency to crab or belittle him. He is the most splendid and awful of Homer's Olympians.

The case of Pallas Athena is even simpler, though it leads to a somewhat surprising result. What Apollo is to Ionia that, and more, Athena is to Athens. There are doubtless foreign elements in Athena, some Cretan

---

[1] *Themis*, p. 439 f. Cf. ὁ Ἀγοραῖος. Other explanations of the name in Gruppe, p. 1224 f., notes.

[2] Hdt. i. 147 ; Plato, *Euthyd.* 302 c : *Socrates.* 'No Ionian recognizes a Zeus Patrôos ; Apollo is our Patrôos, because he was father of Ion.'

and Ionian, some Northern.[1] But her whole appearance
in history and literature tells the same story as her
name. Athens is her city and she is the goddess of
Athens, the Athena or Athenaia Korê. In Athens she
can be simply ' Parthenos ', the Maiden ; elsewhere
she is the ' Attic ' or ' Athenian Maiden '. As
Glaucopis she is identified or associated with the
Owl that was the sacred bird of Athens. As Pallas she
seems to be a Thunder-maiden, a sort of Keraunia or
bride of Keraunos. A Palladion consists of two
thunder-shields, set one above the other like a figure
8, and we can trace in art-types the development of
this 8 into a human figure. It seems clear that the
old Achaioi cannot have called their warrior-maiden,
daughter of Zeus, by the name Athena or Athenaia.
The Athenian goddess must have come in from
Athenian influence, and it is strange to find how deep
into the heart of the poems that influence must have
reached. If we try to conjecture whose place it is
that Athena has taken, it is worth remarking that her
regular epithet, ' daughter of Zeus ', belongs in Sanskrit
to the Dawn-goddess, Eôs.[2] The transition might
be helped by some touches of the Dawn-goddess
that seem to linger about Athena in myth. The
rising Sun stayed his horses while Athena was born
from the head of Zeus. Also she was born amid
a snow-storm of gold. And Eôs, on the other hand, is,

---

[1] See Gruppe, p. 1206, on the development of his ' Philistine
thunderstorm-goddess '.

[2] Hoffmann, *Gesch. d. griechischen Sprache*, Leipzig, 1911, p. 16.
Cf. Pind. *Ol.* vii. 35 ; Ov. *Metam.* ix. 421 ; xv. 191, 700, &c.

like Athena, sometimes the daughter of the Giant Pallas.[1]

Our three chief Olympians, then, explain themselves very easily. A body of poetry and tradition, in its origin dating from the Achaioi of the Migrations, growing for centuries in the hands of Ionian bards, and reaching its culminating form at Athens, has prominent in it the Achaian Zeus, the Ionian Apollo, the Athenian Korê—the same Korê who descended

---

[1] As to the name, Ἀθηναία is of course simply 'Athenian'; the shorter and apparently original form Ἀθάνα, Ἀθήνη is not so clear, but it seems most likely to mean 'Attic'. Cf. Meister, *Gr. Dial.* ii. 290. He classes under the head of Oertliche Bestimmungen : ἁ θεὸς ἁ Παφία (Collitz and Bechtel, *Sammlung der griechischen Dialekt-Inschriften*, 2, 3, 14ᵃ, ᵇ, 15, 16). 'In Paphos selbst hiess die Göttin nur ἁ θεός oder ἁ Ϝάνασσα;—ἁ θιὸς ἁ Γολγία (61)—ἁ θιὸς ἁ Ἀθάνα ἁ πὲρ Ἠδάλιον (60, 27, 28), 'die Göttin, die Athenische, die über Edalion (waltet)'; 'Ἀθ-άνα ist, wie J. Baunack (*Studia Nicolaitana*, s. 27) gezeigt hat, das Adjectiv zu (* Ἀσσ-ίς ' Seeland') : Ἀττ-ίς; Ἀτθ-ίς; * Ἀθ-ίς; also Ἀθ-άνα = Ἀττ-ική, Ἀθ-ῆναι ursprünglich Ἀθ-ῆναι κῶμαι.' Other derivations in Gruppe, p. 1194. Or again αἱ Ἀθῆναι may be simply 'the place where the Athenas are', like οἱ ἰχθύες, the fish-market; 'the Athenas' would be statues, like οἱ Ἑρμαῖ—the famous 'Attic Maidens' on the Acropolis. This explanation would lead to some interesting results.

We need not here consider how, partly by identification with other Korae, like Pallas, Onka, &c., partly by a genuine spread of the cult, Athena became prominent in other cities. As to Homer, Athena is far more deeply imbedded in the *Odyssey* than in the *Iliad*. I am inclined to agree with those who believe that our *Odyssey* was very largely composed in Athens, so that in most of the poem Athena is original. (Cf. O. Seeck, *Die Quellen der Odyssee* (1887), pp. 366–420; Mülder, *Die Ilias und ihre Quellen* (1910), pp. 350–5.) In some parts of the *Iliad* the name Athena may well have been substituted for some Northern goddess whose name is now lost.

in person to restore the exiled Pisistratus to his throne.[1]

We need only throw a glance in passing at a few of the other Olympians. Why, for instance, should Poseidon be so prominent? In origin he is a puzzling figure. Besides the Achaean Earth-shaking brother of Zeus in Thessaly there seems to be some Pelasgian or Aegean god present in him. He is closely connected with Libya; he brings the horse from there.[2] At times he exists in order to be defeated; defeated in Athens by Athena, in Naxos by Dionysus, in Aegina by Zeus, in Argos by Hera, in Acrocorinth by Helios though he continues to hold the Isthmus. In Trozen he shares a temple on more or less equal terms with Athena.[3] Even in Troy he is defeated and cast out from the walls his own hands had built.[4] These problems we need not for the present face. By the time that concerns us most the Earth-Shaker is a sea-god, specially important to the sea-peoples of Athens

---

[1] It is worth noting also that this Homeric triad seems also to be recognized as the chief Athenian triad. Plato, *Euthyd.* 302 c, quoted above, continues: *Socrates.* 'We have Zeus with the names Herkeios and Phratrios, but not Patrôos, and Athena Phratria.' *Dionysodorus.* 'Well, that is enough. You have, apparently, Apollo and Zeus and Athena?' *Socrates.* 'Certainly.'—Apollo is put first because he has been accepted as Patrôos. But see *R. G. E.,*[3] p. 49, n.

[2] Ridgeway, *Origin and Influence of the Thoroughbred Horse,* 1905, pp. 287–93; and *Early Age of Greece,* 1901, p. 223.

[3] Cf. Plut. *Q. Conv.* ix. 6; Paus. ii. 1. 6; 4. 6; 15. 5; 30. 6.

[4] So in the non-Homeric tradition, Eur. *Troades* init. In the *Iliad* he is made an enemy of Troy, like Athena, who is none the less the Guardian of the city.

and Ionia. He is the father of Neleus, the ancestor of the Ionian kings. His temple at Cape Mykale is the scene of the Panionia, and second only to Delos as a religious centre of the Ionian tribes. He has intimate relations with Attica too. Besides the ancient contest with Athena for the possession of the land, he appears as the father of Theseus, the chief Athenian hero. He is merged in other Attic heroes, like Aigeus and Erechtheus. He is the special patron of the Athenian knights. Thus his prominence in Homer is very natural.

What of Hermes? His history deserves a long monograph to itself; it is so exceptionally instructive. Originally, outside Homer, Hermes was simply an old upright stone, a pillar furnished with the regular Pelasgian sex-symbol of procreation. Set up over a tomb he is the power that generates new lives, or, in the ancient conception, brings the souls back to be born again. He is the Guide of the Dead, the Psychopompos, the divine Herald between the two worlds. If you have a message for the dead, you speak it to the Herm at the grave. This notion of Hermes as herald may have been helped by his use as a boundary-stone—the Latin *Terminus*. Your boundary-stone is your representative, the deliverer of your message, to the hostile neighbour or alien. If you wish to parley with him, you advance up to your boundary-stone. If you go, as a Herald, peacefully, into his territory, you place yourself under the protection of the same sacred stone, the last sign that remains of your own safe country. If you are killed or wronged, it is he, the immovable Watcher, who will avenge you.

Now this phallic stone post was quite unsuitable to Homer. It was not decent; it was not quite human; and every personage in Homer has to be both. In the *Iliad* Hermes is simply removed, and a beautiful creation or tradition, Iris, the rainbow-goddess, takes his place as the messenger from heaven to earth. In the *Odyssey* he is admitted, but so changed and castigated that no one would recognize the old Herm in the beautiful and gracious youth who performs the gods' messages. I can only detect in his language one possible trace of his old Pelasgian character.[1]

Pausanias knew who worked the transformation. In speaking of Hermes among the other ' Workers ', who were ' pillars in square form ', he says, ' As to Hermes, the poems of Homer have given currency to the report that he is a servant of Zeus and leads down the spirits of the departed to Hades '.[2] In the magic papyri Hermes returns to something of his old functions; he is scarcely to be distinguished from the Agathos Daimon. But thanks to Homer he is purified of his old phallicism.

Hera, too, the wife of Zeus, seems to have a curious past behind her. She has certainly ousted the original wife, Dione, whose worship continued unchallenged in far Dodona, from times before Zeus descended upon Greek lands. When he invaded Thessaly he seems to have left Dione behind and wedded the Queen of the conquered territory. Hera's permanent epithet is ' Argeia ', ' Argive '. She is the Argive Korê, or Year-

---

[1] *Od.* θ 339 ff.
[2] See Paus. viii. 32. 4. *Themis*, pp. 295, 296.

Maiden, as Athena is the Attic, Cypris the Cyprian. But Argos in Homer denotes two different places, a watered plain in the Peloponnese and a watered plain in Thessaly. Hera was certainly the chief goddess of Peloponnesian Argos in historic times, and had brought her consort Herakles [1] along with her, but at one time she seems to have belonged to the Thessalian Argos. She helped Thessalian Jason to launch the ship *Argo*, and they launched it from Thessalian Pagasae. In the Argonautica she is a beautiful figure, gracious and strong, the lovely patroness of the young hero. No element of strife is haunting her. But in the *Iliad* for some reason she is unpopular. She is a shrew, a scold, and a jealous wife. Why? Miss Harrison suggests that the quarrel with Zeus dates from the time of the invasion, when he was the conquering alien and she the native queen of the land.[2] It may be, too, that the Ionian poets who respected their own Apollo and Athena and Poseidon, regarded Hera as representing some race or tribe that they disliked. A goddess of Dorian Argos might be as disagreeable as a Dorian. It seems to be for some reason like this that Aphrodite, identified with Cyprus or some centre among Oriental

---

[1] For the connexion of Ἥρα ἥρως Ἡρακλῆς (Ἡρύκαλος in Sophron, fr. 142 K) see especially A. B. Cook, *Class. Review*, 1906, pp. 365 and 416. The name Ἥρα seems probably to be an ' ablaut ' form of ὥρα: cf. phrases like Ἥρα τελεία. Other literature in Gruppe, pp. 452, 1122.

[2] *Prolegomena*, p. 315, referring to H. D. Müller, *Mythologie d. gr. Stämme*, pp. 249–55. Another view is suggested by Mülder, *Die Ilias und ihre Quellen*, p. 136. The jealous Hera comes from the Heracles-saga, in which the wife hated the bastard.

barbarians, is handled with so much disrespect ; that
Ares, the Thracian Kouros, a Sun-god and War-god, is
treated as a mere bully and coward and general pest.[1]

There is not much faith in these gods, as they appear
to us in the Homeric Poems, and not much respect,
except perhaps for Apollo and Athena and Poseidon.
The buccaneer kings of the Heroic Age, cut loose from
all local and tribal pieties, intent only on personal gain
and glory, were not the people to build up a powerful
religious faith. They left that, as they left agriculture
and handiwork, to the nameless common folk.[2] And
it was not likely that the bards of cultivated and
scientific Ionia should waste much religious emotion
on a system which was clearly meant more for romance
than for the guiding of life.

Yet the power of romance is great. In the memory
of Greece the kings and gods of the Heroic Age were
transfigured. What had been really an age of bucca-
neering violence became in memory an age of chivalry
and splendid adventure. The traits that were at all
tolerable were idealized ; those that were intolerable
were either expurgated, or, if that was impossible,
were mysticized and explained away. And the savage
old Olympians became to Athens and the mainland of
Greece from the sixth century onward emblems of high
humanity and religious reform.

---

[1] P. Gardner, in *Numismatic Chronicle*, N.S. xx, ' Ares as a Sun-
God '.

[2] Chadwick, *Heroic Age*, especially pp. 414, 459–63.

II. *The Religious Value of the Olympians*

Now to some people this statement may seem a wilful paradox, yet I believe it to be true. The Olympian religion, radiating from Homer at the Panathenaea, produced what I will venture to call exactly a religious reformation. Let us consider how, with all its flaws and falsehoods, it was fitted to attempt such a work.

In the first place the Poems represent an Achaian tradition, the tradition of a Northern conquering race, organized on a patriarchal monogamous system vehemently distinct from the matrilinear customs of the Aegean or Hittite races, with their polygamy and polyandry, their agricultural rites, their sex-emblems and fertility goddesses. Contrast for a moment the sort of sexless Valkyrie who appears in the *Iliad* under the name of Athena with the Korê of Ephesus, strangely called Artemis, a shapeless fertility figure, covered with innumerable breasts. That suggests the contrast that I mean.

Secondly, the poems are by tradition aristocratic; they are the literature of chieftains, alien to low popular superstition. True, the poems as we have them are not Court poems. That error ought not to be so often repeated. As we have them they are poems recited at a Panegyris, or public festival. But they go back in ultimate origin to something like lays sung in a royal hall. And the contrast between the Homeric gods and the gods found outside Homer is well compared by Mr. Chadwick [1] to the difference

[1] Chap. xviii.

between the gods of the Edda and the historical traces of religion outside the Edda. The gods who feast with Odin in Asgard, forming an organized community or *comitatus*, seem to be the gods of the kings, distinct from the gods of the peasants, cleaner and more war-like and lordlier, though in actual religious quality much less vital.

Thirdly, the poems in their main stages are Ionian, and Ionia was for many reasons calculated to lead the forward movement against the 'Urdummheit'. For one thing, Ionia reinforced the old Heroic tradition, in having much the same inward freedom. The Ionians are the descendants of those who fled from the invaders across the sea, leaving their homes, tribes, and tribal traditions. Wilamowitz has well remarked how the imagination of the Greek mainland is dominated by the gigantic sepulchres of unknown kings, which the fugitives to Asia had left behind them and half forgotten.[1]

Again, when the Ionians settled on the Asiatic coasts they were no doubt to some extent influenced, but they were far more repelled by the barbaric tribes of the interior. They became conscious, as we have said, of something that was Hellenic, as distinct from something else that was barbaric, and the Hellenic part of them vehemently rejected what struck them as superstitious, cruel, or unclean. And lastly, we must remember that Ionia was, before the rise of Athens, not only the most imaginative and intellectual part of Greece, but by far the most advanced in knowledge

---

[1] Introduction to his edition of the *Choëphoroe*, p. 9.

and culture. The Homeric religion is a step in the self-realization of Greece, and such self-realization naturally took its rise in Ionia.

Granted, then, that Homer was calculated to produce a kind of religious reformation in Greece, what kind of reformation was it? We are again reminded of St. Paul. It was a move away from the ' beggarly elements ' towards some imagined person behind them. The world was conceived as neither quite without external governance, nor as merely subject to the incursions of *mana* snakes and bulls and thunder-stones and monsters, but as governed by an organized body of personal and reasoning rulers, wise and bountiful fathers, like man in mind and shape, only unspeakably higher.

For a type of this Olympian spirit we may take a phenomenon that has perhaps sometimes wearied us : the reiterated insistence in the reliefs of the best period on the strife of men against centaurs or of gods against giants. Our modern sympathies are apt to side with the giants and centaurs. An age of order likes romantic violence, as landsmen safe in their houses like storms at sea. But to the Greek, this battle was full of symbolical meaning. It is the strife, the ultimate victory, of human intelligence, reason, and gentleness, against what seems at first the overwhelming power of passion and unguided strength. It is Hellas against the brute world.[1]

---

[1] The spirit appears very simply in Eur. *Iph. Taur.* 386 ff., where Iphigenia rejects the gods who demand human sacrifice :

> These tales be false, false as those feastings wild
> Of Tantalus, and gods that tare a child.

The victory of Hellenism over barbarism, of man over beast : that was the aim, but was it ever accomplished ? The Olympian gods as we see them in art appear so calm, so perfect, so far removed from the atmosphere of acknowledged imperfection and spiritual striving, that what I am now about to say may again seem a deliberate paradox. It is nevertheless true that the Olympian Religion is only to the full intelligible and admirable if we realize it as a superb and baffled endeavour, not a *telos* or completion but a movement and effort of life.

We may analyse the movement into three main elements : a moral expurgation of the old rites, an attempt to bring order into the old chaos, and lastly an adaptation to new social needs. We will take the three in order.

In the first place, it gradually swept out of religion, or at least covered with a decent veil, that great mass of rites which was concerned with the Food-supply and the Tribe-supply and aimed at direct stimulation

> This land of murderers to its gods hath given
> Its own lust. Evil dwelleth not in heaven.

Yet just before she has accepted the loves of Zeus and Leto without objection. ' Leto, whom Zeus loved, could never have given birth to such a monster ! ' Cf. Plutarch, *Vit. Pelop.* xxi, where Pelopidas, in rejecting the idea of a human sacrifice, says : ' No high and more than human beings could be pleased with so barbarous and unlawful a sacrifice. It was not the fabled Titans and Giants who ruled the world, but one who was a Father of all gods and men.' Of course, criticism and expurgation of the legends is too common to need illustration. See especially Kaibel, *Daktyloi Idaioi*, 1902, p. 512.

of generative processes.[1] It left only a few reverent
and mystic rituals, a few licensed outbursts of riotous
indecency in comedy and the agricultural festivals. It
swept away what seems to us a thing less dangerous,
a large part of the worship of the dead. Such worship,
our evidence shows us, gave a loose rein to superstition.
To the Olympian movement it was vulgar, it was semi-
barbarous, it was often bloody. We find that it has
almost disappeared from Homeric Athens at a time
when the monuments show it still flourishing in un-
Homeric Sparta. The Olympian movement swept
away also, at least for two splendid centuries, the
worship of the man-god, with its diseased atmosphere
of megalomania and blood-lust.[2] These things return
with the fall of Hellenism ; but the great period, as it
urges man to use all his powers of thought, of daring
and endurance, of social organization, so it bids him
remember that he is a man like other men, subject to the
same laws and bound to reckon with the same death.

So much for the moral expurgation : next for the
bringing of intellectual order. To parody the words
of Anaxagoras, ' In the early religion all things were
together, till the Homeric system came and arranged
them '.

We constantly find in the Greek pantheon beings
who can be described as πολλῶν ὀνομάτων μορφὴ μία,
' one form of many names '. Each tribe, each little
community, sometimes one may almost say each caste

---

[1] Aristophanes did much to reduce this element in comedy ; see
Clouds, 537 ff. : also *Albany Review*, 1907, p. 201.

[2] *R. G. E.*,[3] p. 139 f.

—the Children of the Bards, the Children of the Potters—had its own special gods. Now as soon as there was any general ' Sunoikismos ' or ' Settling-together ', any effective surmounting of the narrowest local barriers, these innumerable gods tended to melt into one another. Under different historical circumstances this process might have been carried resolutely through and produced an intelligible pantheon in which each god had his proper function and there was no overlapping—one Korê, one Kouros, one Sun-God, and so on. But in Greece that was impossible. Imaginations had been too vivid, and local types had too often become clearly personified and differentiated. The Maiden of Athens, Athena, did no doubt absorb some other Korai, but she could not possibly combine with her of Cythêra or Cyprus, or Ephesus, nor with the Argive Korê or the Delian or the Brauronian. What happened was that the infinite cloud of Maidens was greatly reduced and fell into four or five main types. The Korai of Cyprus, Cythêra, Corinth, Eryx, and some other places were felt to be one, and became absorbed in the great figure of Aphrodite. Artemis absorbed a quantity more, including those of Delos and Brauron, of various parts of Arcadia and Sparta, and even, as we saw, the fertility Korê of Ephesus. Doubtless she and the Delian were originally much closer together, but the Delian differentiated towards ideal virginity, the Ephesian towards ideal fruitfulness. The Kouroi, or Youths, in the same way were absorbed into some half-dozen great mythological shapes, Apollo, Ares, Hermes, Dionysus, and the like.

As so often in Greek development, we are brought up against the immense formative power of fiction or romance. The simple Korê or Kouros was a figure of indistinct outline with no history or personality. Like the Roman functional gods, such beings were hardly persons; they melted easily one into another. But when the Greek imagination had once done its work upon them, a figure like Athena or Aphrodite had become, for all practical purposes, a definite person, almost as definite as Achilles or Odysseus, as Macbeth or Falstaff. They crystallize hard. They will no longer melt or blend, at least not at an ordinary temperature. In the fourth and third centuries we hear a great deal about the gods all being one, 'Zeus the same as Hades, Hades as Helios, Helios the same as Dionysus',[1] but the amalgamation only takes place in the white heat of ecstatic philosophy or the rites of religious mysticism.

The best document preserved to us of this attempt to bring order into Chaos is the poetry of Hesiod. There are three poems, all devoted to this object, composed perhaps under the influence of Delphi and certainly under that of Homer, and trying in a quasi-Homeric dialect and under a quasi-Olympian system to bring together vast masses of ancient theology and folk-lore and scattered tradition. The *Theogony* attempts to make a pedigree and hierarchy of the Gods; *The Catalogue of Women* and the *Eoiai*,

---

[1] Justin, *Cohort.* c. 15. But such pantheistic language is common in Orphic and other mystic literature. See the fragments of the Orphic Διαθῆκαι (pp. 144 ff. in Abel's *Hymni*).

preserved only in scanty fragments, attempt to fix in canonical form the cloudy mixture of dreams and boasts and legends and hypotheses by which most royal families in central Greece recorded their descent from a traditional ancestress and a conjectural God. The *Works and Days* form an attempt to collect and arrange the rules and tabus relating to agriculture. The work of Hesiod as a whole is one of the most valiant failures in literature. The confusion and absurdity of it are only equalled by its strange helpless beauty and its extraordinary historical interest. The Hesiodic system when compared with that of Homer is much more explicit, much less expurgated, infinitely less accomplished and tactful. At the back of Homer lay the lordly warrior-gods of the Heroic Age, at the back of Hesiod the crude and tangled superstitions of the peasantry of the mainland. Also the Hesiodic poets worked in a comparatively backward and unenlightened atmosphere, the Homeric were exposed to the full light of Athens.

The third element in this Homeric reformation is an attempt to make religion satisfy the needs of a new social order. The earliest Greek religion was clearly based on the tribe, a band of people, all in some sense kindred and normally living together, people with the same customs, ancestors, initiations, flocks and herds and fields. This tribal and agricultural religion can hardly have maintained itself unchanged at the great Aegean centres, like Cnossus and Mycenae.[1] It

---

[1] I have not attempted to consider the Cretan cults. They lie historically outside the range of these essays, and I am not competent

certainly did not maintain itself among the marauding chiefs of the heroic age. It bowed its head beneath the sceptre of its own divine kings and the armed heel of its northern invaders, only to appear again almost undamaged and unimproved when the kings were fallen and the invaders sunk into the soil like storms of destructive rain.

But it no longer suited its environment. In the age of the migrations the tribes had been broken, scattered, re-mixed. They had almost ceased to exist as important social entities. The social unit which had taken their place was the political community of men, of whatever tribe or tribes, who were held together in times of danger and constant war by means of a common circuit-wall, a Polis.[1] The idea of the tribe remained. In the earliest classical period we find every Greek city still nominally composed of tribes, but the tribes are fictitious. The early city-makers could still only conceive of society on a tribal basis. Every local or accidental congregation of

to deal with evidence that is purely archaeological. But in general I imagine the Cretan religion to be a development from the religion described in my first essay, affected both by the change in social structure from village to sea-empire and by foreign, especially Egyptian, influences. No doubt the Achaean gods were influenced on their side by Cretan conceptions, though perhaps not so much as Ionia was. Cf. the Cretan influences in Ionian vase-painting, and e.g. A. B. Cook on ' Cretan Axe-cult outside Crete ', *Transactions of the Third International Congress for the History of Religion*, ii. 184. See also Sir A. Evans's striking address on ' The Minoan and Mycenaean Element in Hellenic Life ', *J. H. S.* xxxii. 277–97.

[1] See *R. G. E.*,[3] p. 58 f.

people who wish to act together have to invent an imaginary common ancestor. The clash between the old tribal traditions that have lost their meaning, though not their sanctity, and the new duties imposed by the actual needs of the Polis, leads to many strange and interesting compromises. The famous constitution of Cleisthenes shows several. An old proverb expresses well the ordinary feeling on the subject :

ὡς κε πόλις ῥέξειε, νόμος δ' ἀρχαῖος ἄριστος.

' Whatever the City may do ; but the old custom is the best.'

Now in the contest between city and tribe, the Olympian gods had one great negative advantage. They were not tribal or local, and all other gods were. They were by this time international, with no strong roots anywhere except where one of them could be identified with some native god ; they were full of fame and beauty and prestige. They were ready to be made ' Poliouchoi ', ' City-holders ', of any particular city, still more ready to be ' Hellânioi ', patrons of al Hellas.

In the working out of these three aims the Olympian religion achieved much : in all three it failed. The moral expurgation failed owing to the mere force of inertia possessed by old religious traditions and local cults. We must remember how weak any central government was in ancient civilization. The power and influence of a highly civilized society were apt to end a few miles outside its city wall. All through the backward parts of Greece obscene and cruel rites lingered on, the darker and worse the further they were removed from the full light of Hellenism.

But in this respect the Olympian Religion did not merely fail : it did worse. To make the elements of a nature-religion human is inevitably to make them vicious. There is no great moral harm in worshipping a thunder-storm, even though the lightning strikes the good and evil quite recklessly. There is no need to pretend that the Lightning is exercising a wise and righteous choice. But when once you worship an imaginary quasi-human being who throws the lightning, you are in a dilemma. Either you have to admit that you are worshipping and flattering a being with no moral sense, because he happens to be dangerous, or else you have to invent reasons for his wrath against the people who happen to be struck. And they are pretty sure to be bad reasons. The god, if personal, becomes capricious and cruel.

When the Ark of Israel was being brought back from the Philistines, the cattle slipped by the threshing floor of Nachon, and the holy object was in danger of falling. A certain Uzzah, as we all know, sprang forward to save it and was struck dead for his pains. Now, if he was struck dead by the sheer holiness of the tabu object, the holiness stored inside it like so much electricity, his death was a misfortune, an interesting accident, and no more.[1] But when it is made into the deliberate act of an anthropomorphic god, who

[1] 2 Sam. vi 6. See S. Reinach, *Orpheus*, p. 5 (English Translation, p. 4).

strikes a well-intentioned man dead in explosive rage
for a very pardonable mistake, a dangerous element
has been introduced into the ethics of that religion.
A being who is the moral equal of man must not behave
like a charge of dynamite.

Again, to worship emblems of fertility and generation,
as was done in agricultural rites all through the Aegean
area, is in itself an intelligible and not necessarily
a degrading practice. But when those emblems are
somehow humanized, and the result is an anthropomorphic god of enormous procreative power and innumerable amours, a religion so modified has received
a death-blow. The step that was meant to soften its
grossness has resulted in its moral degradation. This
result was intensified by another well-meant effort at
elevation. The leading tribes of central Greece were,
as we have mentioned, apt to count their descent from
some heroine-ancestress. Her consort was sometimes
unknown and, in a matrilinear society, unimportant.
Sometimes he was a local god or river. When the
Olympians came to introduce some order and unity
among these innumerable local gods, the original tribal
ancestor tended, naturally enough, to be identified
with Zeus, Apollo, or Poseidon. The unfortunate
Olympians, whose system really aimed at purer morals
and condemned polygamy and polyandry, are left with
a crowd of consorts that would put Solomon to shame.

Thus a failure in the moral expurgation was deepened
by a failure in the attempt to bring intellectual order
into the welter of primitive gods. The only satisfactory end of that effort would have been monotheism.

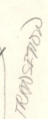

If Zeus had only gone further and become completely, once and for all, the father of all life, the scandalous stories would have lost their point and meaning. It is curious how near to monotheism, and to monotheism of a very profound and impersonal type, the real religion of Greece came in the sixth and fifth centuries. Many of the philosophers, Xenophanes, Parmenides, and others, asserted it clearly or assumed it without hesitation. Aeschylus, Euripides, Plato, in their deeper moments point the same road. Indeed a metaphysician might hold that their theology is far deeper than that to which we are accustomed, since they seem not to make any particular difference between οἱ θεοί and ὁ θεός or τὸ θεῖον. They do not instinctively suppose that the human distinctions between 'he' and 'it', or between 'one' and 'many', apply to the divine. Certainly Greek monotheism, had it really carried the day, would have been a far more philosophic thing than the tribal and personal monotheism of the Hebrews. But unfortunately too many hard-caked superstitions, too many tender and sensitive associations, were linked with particular figures in the pantheon or particular rites which had brought the worshippers religious peace. If there had been some Hebrew prophets about, and a tyrant or two, progressive and bloody-minded, to agree with them, polytheism might perhaps actually have been stamped out in Greece at one time. But Greek thought, always sincere and daring, was seldom brutal, seldom ruthless or cruel. The thinkers of the great period felt their own way gently to the Holy of Holies, and did not try to compel others to take the same way. Greek theology, whether popular or philosophical seldom denied any god, seldom forbade any worship. What it tried to do was to identify every new god with some aspect of one of the old ones, and the result was naturally confusion. Apart from the Epicurean school, which though powerful was always unpopular, the religious thought of later antiquity for the most part took refuge in a sort of apotheosis of good taste, in which the great care was not to hurt other people's feelings, or else it collapsed into helpless mysticism.

The attempt to make Olympianism a religion of the Polis failed also. The Olympians did not belong to any particular city : they were too universal ; and no particular city had a very positive faith in them. The actual Polis was real and tangible, the Homeric gods a little alien and literary. The City herself was a most real power ; and the true gods of the City, who had grown out of the soil and the wall, were simply the City herself in her eternal and personal aspect, as mother and guide and lawgiver, the worshipped and beloved being whom each citizen must defend even to the death. As the Kouros of his day emerged from the social group of Kouroi, or the Aphiktor from the band of suppliants, in like fashion ἡ Πολιάς or ὁ Πολιεύς emerged as a personification or projection of the city. ἡ Πολιάς in Athens was of course Athena ; ὁ Πολιεύς might as well be called Zeus as anything else. In reality such beings fall into the same class as the hero Argos or ' Korinthos son of Zeus '. The City worship was narrow ; yet to broaden it was, except in some rare minds, to sap its life. The ordinary man finds it impossible to love his next-door neighbours except by siding with them against the next-door-but-one.

It proved difficult even in a city like Athens to have gods that would appeal to the loyalty of all Attica. On the Acropolis at Athens there seem originally to have been Athena and some Kouros corresponding with her, some Waterer of the earth, like Erechtheus. Then as Attica was united and brought under the lead of its central city, the gods of the outlying districts began to claim places on the Acropolis. Pallas, the thunder-maid of Pallene in the south, came to form a joint personality with Athena. Oinoe, a town in the north-east, on the way from Delos to Delphi, had for its special god a ' Pythian Apollo ' ; when Oinoe became Attic a place for the Pythian Apollo had to be found on the Acropolis. Dionysus came from Eleutherae, Demeter and Korê from Eleusis, Theseus himself perhaps from Marathon or even from Trozên. They were all given official residences on Athena's rock, and Athens in return sent out Athena to new temples built for her in Prasiae and Sunion and various colonies.[1] This development came step by step and grew out of real worships. It was quite different from the wholesale adoption of a body of non-national, poetical gods : yet even this develop-ment was too artificial, too much stamped with the marks of expediency and courtesy and compromise. It could not live. The personalities of such gods vanish away ; their prayers become prayers to ' all

[1] Cf. Sam Wide in Gercke and Norden's *Handbuch*, ii. 217-19.

gods and goddesses of the City '—θεοῖς καὶ θεῇσι πᾶσι
καὶ πάσῃσι; those who remain, chiefly Athena and
Theseus, only mean Athens.

What then, amid all this failure, did the Olympian
religion really achieve? First, it debarbarized the
worship of the leading states of Greece—not of all
Greece, since antiquity had no means of spreading
knowledge comparable to ours. It reduced the horrors
of the 'Urdummheit', for the most part, to a romantic memory, and made religion no longer a mortal
danger to humanity. Unlike many religious systems, it
generally permitted progress; it encouraged not only
the obedient virtues but the daring virtues as well.
It had in it the spirit that saves from disaster, that
knows itself fallible and thinks twice before it hates
and curses and persecutes. It wrapped religion in
Sophrosynê.

Again, it worked for concord and fellow-feeling
throughout the Greek communities. It is, after all,
a good deal to say, that in Greek history we find
almost no warring of sects, no mutual tortures or even
blasphemies. With many ragged edges, with many
weaknesses, it built up something like a united Hellenic
religion to stand against the 'beastly devices of the
heathen'. And after all, if we are inclined on the
purely religious side to judge the Olympian system
harshly, we must not forget its sheer beauty. Truth,
no doubt, is greater than beauty. But in many matters
beauty can be attained and truth cannot. All we know
is that when the best minds seek for truth the result
is apt to be beautiful. It was a great thing that men

should envisage the world as governed, not by Giants
and Gorgons and dealers in eternal torture, but by
some human and more than human Understanding
(Ξύνεσις),[1] by beings of quiet splendour like many a
classical Zeus and Hermes and Demeter. If Olympianism was not a religious faith, it was at least a vital
force in the shaping of cities and societies which remain
after two thousand years a type to the world of beauty
and freedom and high endeavour. Even the stirring
of its ashes, when they seemed long cold, had power
to produce something of the same result; for the
classicism of the Italian Renaissance is a child, however
fallen, of the Olympian spirit.

Of course, I recognize that beauty is not the same as
faith. There is, in one sense, far more faith in some
hideous miracle-working icon which sends out starving
peasants to massacre Jews than in the Athena of Phidias.
Yet, once we have rid our minds of trivial mythology,
there is religion in Athena also. Athena is an ideal,
an ideal and a mystery; the ideal of wisdom, of incessant labour, of almost terrifying purity, seen through
the light of some mystic and spiritual devotion like, but
transcending, the love of man for woman. Or, if the
way of Athena is too hard for us common men, it is not
hard to find a true religious ideal in such a figure as
Persephone. In Persephone there is more of pathos and

---

[1] The Ξύνεσις in which the Chorus finds it hard to believe, *Hippolytus*, 1105. Cf. *Iph. Aul.* 394, 1189; *Herc.* 655; also the ideas in
Suppl. 203, Eur. Fr. 52, 9, where Ξύνεσις is implanted in man by a special
grace of God. The gods are ξυνετοί, but of course Euripides goes too
far in actually praying to Ξύνεσις, Ar. *Frogs*, 893.

of mystery. She has more recently entered the calm ranks of Olympus ; the old liturgy of the dying and re-risen Year-bride still clings to her. If Religion is that which brings us into relation with the great world-forces, there is the very heart of life in this home-coming Bride of the underworld, life with its broken hopes, its disaster, its new-found spiritual joy : life seen as Mother and Daughter, not a thing continuous and unchanging but shot through with parting and death, life as a great love or desire ever torn asunder and ever renewed.

' But stay,' a reader may object : ' is not this the Persephone, the Athena, of modern sentiment ? Are these figures really the goddesses of the *Iliad* and of Sophocles ? ' The truth is, I think, that they are neither the one nor the other. They are the goddesses of ancient reflection and allegory ; the goddesses, that is, of the best and most characteristic worship that these idealized creations awakened. What we have treated hitherto as the mortal weakness of the Olympians, the fact that they have no roots in any particular soil, little hold on any definite primeval cult, has turned out to be their peculiar strength. We must not think of allegory as a late post-classical phenomenon in Greece. It begins at least as early as Pythagoras and Heraclitus, perhaps as early as Hesiod ; for Hesiod seems sometimes to be turning allegory back into myth. The Olympians, cut loose from the soil, enthroned only in men's free imagination, have two special regions which they have made their own : mythology and allegory. The mythology drops for the most part very early out

N

of practical religion. Even in Homer we find it expurgated; in Pindar, Aeschylus, and Xenophanes it is expurgated, denied and allegorized. The myths survive chiefly as material for literature, the shapes of the gods themselves chiefly as material for art. They are both of them objects not of belief but of imagination. Yet when the religious imagination of Greece deepens it twines itself still round these gracious and ever-moving shapes; the Zeus of Aeschylus moves on into the Zeus of Plato or of Cleanthes or of Marcus Aurelius. Hermes, Athena, Apollo, all have their long spiritual history. They are but little impeded by the echoes of the old frivolous mythology; still less by any local roots or sectional prejudices or compulsory details of ritual. As the more highly educated mind of Greece emerged from a particular, local, tribal, conception of religion, the old denationalized Olympians were ready to receive her.

The real religion of the fifth century was, as we have said, a devotion to the City itself. It is expressed often in Aeschylus and Sophocles, again and again with more discord and more criticism in Euripides and Plato; for the indignant blasphemies of the Gorgias and the Troades bear the same message as the ideal patriotism of the Republic. It is expressed best perhaps, and that without mention of the name of a single god, in the great Funeral Speech of Pericles. It is higher than most modern patriotism because it is set upon higher ideals. It is more fervid because the men practising it lived habitually nearer to the danger-point, and, when they spoke of dying for the City, spoke of a thing they had faced last week and might face again to-morrow. It was more religious because of the unconscious mysticism in which it is clothed even by such hard heads as Pericles and Thucydides, the mysticism of men in the presence of some fact for which they have no words great enough. Yet for all its intensity it was condemned by its mere narrowness. By the fourth century the average Athenian must have recognized what philosophers had recognized long before, that a religion, to be true, must be universal and not the privilege of a particular people. As soon as the Stoics had proclaimed the world to be ' one great City of gods and men ', the only Gods with which Greece could satisfactorily people that City were the idealized band of the old Olympians.

They are artists' dreams, ideals, allegories ; they are symbols of something beyond themselves. They are Gods of half-rejected tradition, of unconscious make-believe, of aspiration. They are gods to whom doubtful philosophers can pray, with all a philosopher's due caution, as to so many radiant and heart-searching hypotheses. They are not gods in whom any one believes as a hard fact. Does this condemn them ? Or is it just the other way ? Is it perhaps that one difference between Religion and Superstition lies exactly in this, that Superstition degrades its worship by turning its beliefs into so many statements of brute fact, on which it must needs act without question, without striving, without any respect for others or any desire for higher or fuller truth ? It is only an accident —though perhaps an invariable accident—that all the

supposed facts are false.   In Religion, however precious
you may consider the truth you draw from it, you
know that it is a truth seen dimly, and possibly seen
by others better than by you.   You know that all your
creeds and definitions are merely metaphors, attempts
to use human language for a purpose for which it was
never made.   Your concepts are, by the nature of
things, inadequate ; the truth is not in you but beyond
you, a thing not conquered but still to be pursued.
Something like this, I take it, was the character of
the Olympian Religion in the higher minds of later
Greece.   Its gods could awaken man's worship and
strengthen his higher aspirations ; but at heart they
knew themselves to be only metaphors.   As the most
beautiful image carved by man was not the god, but
only a symbol, to help towards conceiving the god ; [1]

---

[1] Cf. the beautiful defence of idols by Maximus of Tyre, Or. viii (in
Wilamowitz's *Lesebuch*, ii. 338 ff.).   I quote the last paragraph :

' God Himself, the father and fashioner of all that is, older than the
Sun or the Sky, greater than time and eternity and all the flow of being,
is unnameable by any lawgiver, unutterable by any voice, not to be
seen by any eye.   But we, being unable to apprehend His essence, use
the help of sounds and names and pictures, of beaten gold and ivory
and silver, of plants and rivers, mountain-peaks and torrents, yearning
for the knowledge of Him, and in our weakness naming all that is
beautiful in this world after His nature—just as happens to earthly
lovers.   To them the most beautiful sight will be the actual lineaments
of the beloved, but for remembrance' sake they will be happy in the
sight of a lyre, a little spear, a chair, perhaps, or a running-ground, or
anything in the world that wakens the memory of the beloved.   Why
should I further examine and pass judgement about Images ?   Let
men know what is divine (τὸ θεῖον γένος), let them know : that is all.
If a Greek is stirred to the remembrance of God by the art of Pheidias,

so the god himself, when conceived, was not the reality but only a symbol to help towards conceiving the reality. That was the work set before them. Meantime they issued no creeds that contradicted knowledge, no commands that made man sin against his own inner light.

an Egyptian by paying worship to animals, another man by a river, another by fire—I have no anger for their divergences ; only let them know, let them love, let them remember.'

III

THE GREAT SCHOOLS OF THE
FOURTH CENTURY, B. C.

III

THE GREAT SCHOOLS OF THE
FOURTH CENTURY, B.C.

THERE is a passage in Xenophon describing how, one summer night, in 405 B.C., people in Athens heard a cry of wailing, an *oimôgê*, making its way up between the long walls from the Piraeus, and coming nearer and nearer as they listened. It was the news of the final disaster of Kynoskephalai, brought at midnight to the Piraeus by the galley Paralos. 'And that night no one slept. They wept for the dead, but far more bitterly for themselves, when they reflected what things they had done to the people of Mêlos, when taken by siege, to the people of Histiaea, and Skîonê and Torônê and Aegîna, and many more of the Hellenes.' [1]

The echo of that lamentation seems to ring behind most of the literature of the fourth century, and not the Athenian literature alone. Defeat can on occasion leave men their self-respect or even their pride ; as it did after Chaeronea in 338 and after the Chremonidean War in 262, not to speak of Thermopylae. But the defeat of 404 not only left Athens at the mercy of her enemies. It stripped her of those things of which she had been inwardly most proud ; her 'wisdom', her high civilization, her leadership of all that was most

---

[1] *Hellen.* ii. 2, 3.

Hellenic in Hellas. The ' Beloved City ' of Pericles
had become a tyrant, her nature poisoned by war, her
government a by-word in Greece for brutality. And
Greece as a whole felt the tragedy of it. It is curious
how this defeat of Athens by Sparta seems to have been
felt abroad as a defeat for Greece itself and for the
hopes of the Greek city state. The fall of Athens
mattered more than the victory of Lysander. Neither
Sparta nor any other city ever attempted to take her
place. And no writer after the year 400 speaks of any
other city as Pericles used to speak of fifth-century
Athens, not even Polybius 250 years later, when he
stands amazed before the solidity and the ' fortune '
of Rome.

The city state, the Polis, had concentrated upon
itself almost all the loyalty and the aspirations of the
Greek mind. It gave security to life. It gave meaning to religion. And in the fall of Athens it had
failed. In the third century, when things begin to
recover, we find on the one hand the great military
monarchies of Alexander's successors, and on the
other, a number of federations of tribes, which were
generally strongest in the backward regions where
the city state had been least developed. Τὸ κοινὸν
τῶν Αἰτωλῶν or τῶν Ἀχαιῶν had become more
important than Athens or Corinth, and Sparta was
only strong by means of a League.[1] By that time the
Polis was recognized as a comparatively weak social
organism, capable of very high culture but not quite
able, as the Covenant of the League of Nations

[1] Cf. Tarn, *Antigonus Gonatas*, p. 52, and authorities there quoted.

expresses it, ' to hold its own under the strenuous conditions of modern life'. Besides, it was not now ruled by the best citizens. The best had turned away from politics.

This great discouragement did not take place at a blow. Among the practical statesmen probably most did not form any theory about the cause of the failure but went on, as practical statesmen must, doing as best they could from difficulty to difficulty. But many saw that the fatal danger to Greece was disunion, as many see it in Europe now. When Macedon proved indisputably stronger than Athens Isocrates urged Philip to accept the leadership of Greece against the barbarian and against barbarism. He might thus both unite the Greek cities and also evangelize the world. Lysias, the democratic and anti-Spartan orator, had been groping for a similar solution as early as 384 B.C., and was prepared to make an even sharper sacrifice for it. He appealed at Olympia for a crusade of all the free Greek cities against Dionysius of Syracuse, and begged Sparta herself to lead it. The Spartans are ' of right the leaders of Hellas by their natural nobleness and their skill in war. They alone live still in a city unsacked, unwalled, unconquered, uncorrupted by faction, and have followed always the same modes of life. They have been the saviours of Hellas in the past, and one may hope that their freedom will be everlasting.' [1] A great and generous change in one who had ' learned by suffering ' in the Peloponnesian War. Others no doubt merely gave their submission to the

[1] Lysias, xxxiii.

stronger powers that were now rising. There were openings for counsellors, for mercenary soldiers, for court savants and philosophers and poets, and, of course, for agents in every free city who were prepared for one motive or another not to kick against the pricks. And there were always also those who had neither learned nor forgotten, the unrepentant idealists ; too passionate or too heroic or, as some will say, too blind, to abandon their life-long devotion to ' Athens ' or to ' Freedom ' because the world considered such ideals out of date. They could look the ruined Athenians in the face, after the lost battle, and say with Demosthenes, ' Οὐκ ἔστιν, οὐκ ἔστιν ὅπως ἡμάρτετε. It cannot be that you did wrong, it cannot be ! ' [1]

But in practical politics the currents of thought are inevitably limited. It is in philosophy and speculation that we find the richest and most varied reaction to the Great Failure. It takes different shapes in those writers, like Plato and Xenophon, who were educated in the fifth century and had once believed in the Great City, and those whose whole thinking life belonged to the time of disillusion.

Plato was disgusted with democracy and with Athens, but he retained his faith in the city, if only the city could be set on the right road. There can be little doubt that he attributes to the bad government of the Demos many evils which were really due to extraneous causes or to the mere fallibility of human nature. Still his analysis of democracy is one of the most brilliant things in the history of political theory. It is so acute,

[1] Dem. *Crown*, 208.

so humorous, so affectionate; and at many different ages of the world has seemed like a portrait of the actual contemporary society. Like a modern popular newspaper, Plato's democracy makes it its business to satisfy existing desires and give people a ' good time '. It does not distinguish between higher and lower. Any one man is as good as another, and so is any impulse or any idea. Consequently the commoner have the pull. Even the great democratic statesmen of the past, he now sees, have been ministers to mob desires; they have ' filled the city with harbours and docks and walls and revenues and such-like trash, without Sophrosynê and righteousness '. The sage or saint has no place in practical politics. He would be like a man in a den of wild beasts. Let him and his like seek shelter as best they can, standing up behind some wall while the storm of dust and sleet rages past. The world does not want truth, which is all that he could give it. It goes by appearances and judges its great men with their clothes on and their rich relations round them. After death, the judges will judge them naked, and alone; and then we shall see ![1]

Yet, in spite of all this, the child of the fifth century cannot keep his mind from politics. The speculations which would be scouted by the mass in the market-place can still be discussed with intimate friends and disciples, or written in books for the wise to read. Plato's two longest works are attempts to construct an ideal society; first, what may be called a City of

---

[1] ' Such-like trash ', *Gorgias*, 519 A; dust-storm, *Rep.* vi. 496; clothes, *Gorg.* 523 E; ' democratic man ', *Rep.* viii. 556 ff.

Righteousness, in the *Republic* ; and afterwards in his old age, in the *Laws*, something more like a City of Refuge, uncontaminated by the world ; a little city on a hill-top away in Crete, remote from commerce and riches and the ' bitter and corrupting sea ' which carries them ; a city where life shall move in music and discipline and reverence for the things that are greater than man, and the songs men sing shall be not common songs but the preambles of the city's laws, showing their purpose and their principle ; where no wall will be needed to keep out the possible enemy, because the courage and temperance of the citizens will be wall enough, and if war comes the women equally with the men ' will fight for their young, as birds do '.

This hope is very like despair ; but, such as it is, Plato's thought is always directed towards the city. No other form of social life ever tempts him away, and he anticipates no insuperable difficulty in keeping the city in the right path if once he can get it started right. The first step, the necessary revolution, is what makes the difficulty. And he sees only one way. In real life he had supported the conspiracy of the extreme oligarchs in 404 which led to the rule of the ' Thirty Tyrants ' ; but the experience sickened him of such methods. There was no hope unless, by some lucky combination, a philosopher should become a king or some young king turn philosopher. ' Give me a city governed by a tyrant,' he says in the *Laws*,[1] ' and let the tyrant be young, with a good memory, quick at learning, of high courage, and a generous nature. . . .

[1] *Laws*, 709 E, cf. Letter VII.

And besides, let him have a wise counsellor!' Ironical
fortune granted him an opportunity to try the experiment himself at the court of Syracuse, first with the
elder and then, twenty years later, with the younger
Dionysius (387 and 367 B. C.). It is a story of disappointment, of course; bitter, humiliating and ludi-
crous disappointment, but with a touch of that
sublimity which seems so often to hang about the
errors of the wise. One can study them in Seneca
at the court of Nero, or in Turgot with Louis; not
so well perhaps in Voltaire with Frederick. Plato
failed in his enterprise, but he did keep faith with
the ' Righteous City '.

Another of the Socratic circle turned in a different
direction. Xenophon, an exile from his country,
a brilliant soldier and adventurer as well as a man of
letters, is perhaps the first Greek on record who openly
lost interest in the city. He thought less about cities
and constitutions than about great men and nations,
or generals and armies. To him it was idle to spin
cobweb formations of ideal laws and communities.
Society is right enough if you have a really fine man to
lead it. It may be that his ideal was formed in childhood by stories of Pericles and the great age when
Athens was ' in name a democracy but in truth an
empire of one leading man '. He gave form to his
dream in the *Education of Cyrus*, an imaginary account
of the training which formed Cyrus the Great into an
ideal king and soldier. The *Cyropaedeia* is said to have
been intended as a counterblast to Plato's *Republic*, and
it may have provoked Plato's casual remark in the

Laws that ' Cyrus never so much as touched education '.
No doubt the book suffered in persuasiveness from being
so obviously fictitious.[1] For example, the Cyrus of
Xenophon dies peacefully in his bed after much
affectionate and edifying advice to his family, whereas
all Athens knew from Herodotus how the real Cyrus
had been killed in a war against the Massagetae, and
his head, to slake its thirst for that liquid, plunged into
a wineskin full of human blood. Perhaps also the
monarchical rule of Cyrus was too absolute for Greek
taste. At any rate, later on Xenophon adopted a more
real hero, whom he had personally known and admired.

Agesilaus, king of Sparta, had been taken as a type of
' virtue ' even by the bitter historian Theopompus.
Agesilaus was not only a great general. He knew how
to ' honour the gods, do his duty in the field, and to
practise obedience '. He was true to friend and foe.
On one memorable occasion he kept his word even
to an enemy who had broken his. He enjoined kindness
to enemy captives. When he found small children
left behind by the barbarians in some town that he
occupied—because either their parents or the slave-
merchants had no room for them—he always took care
of them or gave them to guardians of their own race :
' he never let the dogs and wolves get them '. On the
other hand, when he sold his barbarian prisoners he
sent them to market naked, regardless of their modesty,
because it cheered his own soldiers to see how white
and fat they were. He wept when he won a victory

---

[1] Aulus Gellius, xiv. 3 ; Plato, *Laws*, p. 695 ; Xen. *Cyrop*. viii. 7,
compared with *Hdt*. i. 214.

over Greeks ; 'for he loved all Greeks and only hated barbarians'. When he returned home after his successful campaigns, he obeyed the orders of the ephors without question ; his house and furniture were as simple as those of a common man, and his daughter the princess, when she went to and fro to Amyclae, went simply in the public omnibus. He reared chargers and hunting dogs ; the rearing of chariot horses he thought effeminate. But he advised his sister Cynisca about hers, and she won the chariot race at Olympia. ' Have a king like that ', says Xenophon, ' and all will be well. He will govern right ; he will beat your enemies ; and he will set an example of good life. If you want Virtue in the state look for it in a good man, not in a speculative tangle of laws. The Spartan constitution, as it stands, is good enough for any one.'

But it was another of the great Socratics who uttered first the characteristic message of the fourth century, and met the blows of Fortune with a direct challenge. Antisthenes was a man twenty years older than Plato. He had fought at Tanagra in 426 B.C. He had been friends with Gorgias and Prodicus, the great Sophists of the Periclean age. He seems to have been, at any rate till younger and more brilliant men cut him out, the recognized philosophic heir of Socrates.[1] And late in life, after the fall of Athens and the condemnation and death of his master, the man underwent a curious change of heart. He is taunted

---

[1] This is the impression left by Xenophon, especially in the Symposium. Cf. Dümmler, *Antisthenica* (1882) ; *Akademika* (1889). Cf. the *Life of Antisthenes* in Diog. Laert.

more than once with the lateness of his discovery of truth,[1] and with his childish subservience to the old *jeux d'esprit* of the Sceptics which professed to prove the impossibility of knowledge.[2] It seems that he had lost faith in speculation and dialectic and the elaborate superstructures which Plato and others had built upon them ; and he felt, like many moralists after him, a sort of hostility to all knowledge that was not immediately convertible into conduct.

But this scepticism was only part of a general disbelief in the world. Greek philosophy had from the first been concerned with a fundamental question which we moderns seldom put clearly to ourselves. It asked ' What is the Good ? ' meaning thereby ' What is the element of value in life ? ' or ' What should be our chief aim in living ? ' A medieval Christian would have answered without hesitation ' To go to Heaven and not be damned ', and would have been prepared with the necessary prescriptions for attaining that end. But the modern world is not intensely enough con-

---

[1] Γέρων ὀψιμαθής, Plato, *Soph.* 251 B, Isocr. *Helena*, i. 2.

[2] e. g. no combination of subject and predicate can be true because one is different from the other. ' Man ' is ' man ' and ' good ' is ' good ' ; but ' man ' is not ' good '. Nor can ' a horse ' possibly be ' running ' ; they are totally different conceptions. See Plutarch, *adv. Co.* 22, 1 (p. 1119) ; Plato, *Soph.* 251 B ; Arist. *Metaph.* 1024^b 33 ; Top. 104^b 20 ; Plato, *Euthyd.* 285 E. For similar reasons no statement can ever contradict another ; the statements are either the same or not the same ; and if not the same they do not touch. Every object has one λόγος or thing to be said about it ; if you say a different λόγος you are speaking of something else. See especially *Scholia Arist.*, p. 732^a 30 ff. on the passage in the *Metaphysics*, 1024^b 33.

vinced of the reality of Sin and Judgement, Hell and
Heaven, to accept this answer as an authoritative guide
in life, and has not clearly thought out any other. The
ancient Greek spent a great part of his philosophical
activity in trying, without propounding supernatural
rewards and punishments, or at least without laying
stress on them, to think out what the Good of man
really was.

The answers given by mankind to this question seem
to fall under two main heads. Before a battle if both
parties were asked what aim they were pursuing, both
would say without hesitation 'Victory'. After the
battle, the conqueror would probably say that his
purpose was in some way to consolidate or extend his
victory ; but the beaten party, as soon as he had time
to think, would perhaps explain that, after all, victory
was not everything. It was better to have fought for
the right, to have done your best and to have failed,
than to revel in the prosperity of the unjust. And,
since it is difficult to maintain, in the midst of the
triumph of the enemy and your own obvious misery
and humiliation, that all is well and you yourself
thoroughly contented, this second answer easily
develops a third : 'Wait a little, till God's judgement
asserts itself ; and see who has the best of it then ! '
There will be a rich reward hereafter for the suffering
virtuous.

The typical Athenian of the Periclean age would
have been in the first state of mind. His ' good ' would
be in the nature of success : to spread Justice and
Freedom, to make Athens happy and strong and her

laws wise and equal for rich and poor. Antisthenes had fallen violently into the second. He was defeated together with all that he most cared for, and he comforted himself with the thought that nothing matters except to have done your best. As he phrased it *Aretê is the good*, Aretê meaning ' virtue ' or ' goodness ', the quality of a good citizen, a good father, a good dog, a good sword.

The things of the world are vanity, and philosophy as vain as the rest. Nothing but goodness is good ; and the first step towards attaining it is to repent.

There was in Athens a gymnasium built for those who were base-born and could not attend the gymnasia of true citizens. It was called Kynosarges and was dedicated to the great bastard, Heracles. Antisthenes, though he had moved hitherto in the somewhat patrician circle of the Socratics, remembered now that his mother was a Thracian slave, and set up his school in Kynosarges among the disinherited of the earth. He made friends with the ' bad ', who needed befriending. He dressed like the poorest workman. He would accept no disciples except those who could bear hardship, and was apt to drive new-comers away with his stick. Yet he also preached in the streets, both in Athens and Corinth. He preached rhetorically, with parables and vivid emotional phrases, compelling the attention of the crowd. His eloquence was held to be bad style, and it started the form of literature known to the Cynics as χρεία, ' a help ', or διατριβή ' a study ', and by the Christians as ὁμιλία, a ' homily ' or sermon.

This passionate and ascetic old man would have

attracted the interest of the world even more, had it not been for one of his disciples. This was a young man from Sinope, on the Euxine, whom he did not take to at first sight; the son of a disreputable money-changer who had been sent to prison for defacing the coinage. Antisthenes ordered the lad away, but he paid no attention; he beat him with his stick, but he never moved. He wanted 'wisdom', and saw that Antisthenes had it to give. His aim in life was to do as his father had done, to ' deface the coinage ', but on a much larger scale. He would deface all the coinage current in the world. Every conventional stamp was false. The men stamped as generals and kings; the things stamped as honour and wisdom and happiness and riches; all were base metal with lying super-scriptions. All must have the stamp defaced.[1]

This young man was Diogenes, afterwards the most famous of all the Cynics. He started by rejecting all stamps and superscriptions and holding that nothing but *Aretê*, 'worth' or ' goodness ', was good. He rejected tradition. He rejected the current religion and the rules and customs of temple worship. True religion was a thing of the spirit, and needed no forms. He despised divination. He rejected civil life and marriage. He mocked at the general interest in the public games and the respect paid to birth, wealth, or reputation. Let man put aside these delusions and know himself. And for his defences let him arm him-self ' against Fortune with courage, against Convention

---

[1] Τὸ νόμισμα παραχαράττειν : see *Life* in Diog. Laert., fragments in Mullach, vol. ii, and the article in Pauly-Wissowa.

with Nature, against passion with Reason'. For Reason is ' the god within us '.

The salvation for man was to return to Nature, and Diogenes interpreted this return in the simplest and crudest way. He should live like the beasts, like primeval men, like barbarians. Were not the beasts blessed, ῥεῖα ζώοντες like the Gods in Homer? And so, though in less perfection, were primitive men, not vexing their hearts with imaginary sins and conventions. Travellers told of savages who married their sisters, or ate human flesh, or left their dead unburied. Why should they not, if they wished to? No wonder Zeus punished Prometheus the Fire-Bringer, who had brought all this progress upon us and left man civilized and more unhappy than any beast! He deserved his crag and his vulture!

Diogenes took his mission with great earnestness. He was leader in a ' great battle against Pleasures and Desires '. He was ' the servant, the message-bearer, sent by Zeus ', ' the Setter-Free of mankind ' and the ' Healer of passions '.

The life that he personally meant to live, and which he recommended to the wise, was what he called τὸν κυνικὸν βίον, ' a dog's life ', and he himself wished to be ' cynic ' or ' canine '. A dog was brave and faithful; it had no bodily shame, no false theories, and few wants. A dog needed no clothes, no house, no city, no possessions, no titles; what he did need was ' virtue ', Aretê, to catch his prey, to fight wild beasts, and to defend his master; and that he could provide for himself. Diogenes found, of course, that he needed

a little more than an ordinary dog ; a blanket, a wallet
or bowl to hold his food, and a staff ' to beat off dogs
and bad men '. It was the regular uniform of a beggar.
He asked for no house. There was a huge earthen
pitcher—not a tub—outside the Temple of the Great
Mother ; the sort of vessel that was used for burial in
primitive Greece and which still had about it the
associations of a coffin. Diogenes slept there when he
wanted shelter, and it became the nearest approach
to a home that he had. Like a dog he performed any
bodily act without shame, when and where he chose.
He obeyed no human laws because he recognized no
city. He was *Cosmopolìtes*, Citizen of the Universe ;
all men, and all beasts too, were his brothers. He lived
preaching in the streets and begging his bread ;
except that he did not ' beg ', he ' commanded '.
Other folk obeyed his commands because they were
still slaves, while he ' had never been a slave again since
Antisthenes set him free '. He had no fear, because
there was nothing to take from him. Only slaves are
afraid.

Greece rang with stories of his mordant wit, and
every bitter saying became fathered on Diogenes.
Every one knew how Alexander the Great had come
to see the famous beggar and, standing before him
where he sat in the open air, had asked if there was
any boon he could confer on him. ' Yes, move from
between me and the sun.' They knew the king's
saying, ' If I were not Alexander I would be Diogenes ',
and the polite answer ' If I were not Diogenes I would
be Alexander '. The Master of the World and the

Rejector of the World met on an equality. People told too how the Cynic walked about with a lamp in the daytime searching, so he said, 'for a man'. They knew his scorn of the Mysteries with their doctrine of exclusive salvation ; was a thief to be in bliss because he was initiated, while Agesilaus and Epaminondas were in outer darkness ? A few of the stories are more whimsical. A workman carrying a pole accidentally hit Diogenes and cried 'Look out !' 'Why,' said he, ' are you going to hit me again ? '

He had rejected patriotism as he rejected culture. Yet he suffered as he saw Greece under the Macedonians and Greek liberties disappearing. When his death was approaching some disciple asked his wishes about his burial ; 'Let the dogs and wolves have me,' he said ; 'I should like to be of some use to my brothers when I die.' When this request was refused his thoughts turned again to the Macedonian Wars ; ' Bury me face downwards ; everything is soon going to be turned the other way up.'

He remains the permanent and unsurpassed type of one way of grappling with the horror of life. Fear nothing, desire nothing, possess nothing ; and then Life with all its ingenuity of malice cannot disappoint you. If man cannot enter into life nor yet depart from it save through agony and filth, let him learn to endure the one and be indifferent to the other. The watchdog of Zeus on earth has to fulfil his special duty, to warn mankind of the truth and to set slaves free. Nothing else matters.

The criticism of this solution is not that it is selfish.

It is not. The Cynic lives for the salvation of his fellow creatures. And it is worth remembering that before the Roman gladiatorial games were eventually stopped by the self-immolation of the monk Telemachus, two Cynic philosophers had thrown themselves into the arena in the same spirit. Its weakness lies in a false psychology, common to all the world at that time, which imagined that salvation or freedom consists in living utterly without desire or fear, that such a life is biologically possible, and that Diogenes lived it. To a subtler critic it is obvious that Diogenes was a man of very strong and successful ambitions, though his ambitions were different from those of most men. He solved the problem of his own life by following with all the force and courage of his genius a line of conduct which made him, next to Alexander, the most famous man in Greece. To be really without fear or desire would mean death, and to die is not to solve the riddle of living.

The difference between the Cynic view of life and that of Plato's *Republic* is interesting. Plato also rejected the most fundamental conventions of existing society, the accepted methods of government, the laws of property and of marriage, the traditional religion and even the poetry which was a second religion to the Greeks. But he rejected the existing culture only because he wanted it to be better. He condemned the concrete existing city in order to build a more perfect city, to proceed in infinite searching and longing towards the Idea of Good, the Sun of the spiritual universe. Diogenes rejected the civilization which he saw, and admitted the reality of no other. His crude realistic attitude of mind had no use for Plato's 'Ideas'. 'I can see a table,' he said; 'I cannot see Tabularity' ($\tau\rho\alpha\pi\epsilon\zeta\acute{o}\tau\eta\varsigma$). 'I know Athens and Corinth and other cities, and can see that they are all bad. As for the Ideal Society, show it me and I will say what I think.'

In spite of its false psychology the Cynic conception of life had a great effect in Greece. It came almost as a revelation to both men and women [1] and profoundly influenced all the Schools. Here indeed, it seemed, was a way to baffle Fortune and to make one's own soul unafraid. What men wanted was $\tau\grave{o}$ $\theta\alpha\rho\rho\epsilon\hat{\iota}\nu$ ' to be of good cheer'; as we say now, to regain their *morale* after bewildering defeats. The Cynic answer, afterwards corrected and humanized by the Stoics, was to look at life as a long and arduous campaign. The loyal soldier does not trouble about his comfort or his rewards or his pleasures. He obeys his commander's orders without fear or failing, whether they lead to

[1] There were women among the Cynics. 'The doctrine also captured Metrocles' sister, Hipparchia. She loved Crates, his words, and his way of life, and paid no attention to any of her suitors, however rich or highborn or handsome. Crates was everything to her. She threatened her parents that she would commit suicide unless she were given to him. They asked Crates to try to change the girl's mind, and he did all he could to no effect, till at last he put all his possessions on the floor and stood up in front of her. 'Here is your bridegroom; there is his fortune; now think!' The girl made her choice, put on the beggar's garb, and went her ways with Crates. She lived with him openly and went like him to beg food at dinners.' Diog. Laert. vi. 96 ff.

easy victories or merely to wounds, captivity or death. Only Goodness is good, and for the soldier Goodness (ἀρετή) is the doing of Duty. That is his true prize, which no external power can take away from him.

But after all, what is Duty? Diogenes preached ' virtue ' and assumed that his way of life was ' virtue '. But was it really so? And, if so, on what evidence? To live like a beast, to be indifferent to art, beauty, letters, science, philosophy, to the amenities of civic life, to all that raised Hellenic Man above the beast or the savage? How could this be the true end of man? The Stoic School, whose founder, Zeno, was a disciple of old Antisthenes, gradually built up a theory of moral life which has on the whole weathered the storms of time with great success. It largely dominated later antiquity by its imaginative and emotional power. It gave form to the aspirations of early Christianity. It lasts now as the nearest approach to an acceptable system of conduct for those who do not accept revelation, but still keep some faith in the Purpose of Things.

The problem is to combine the absolute value of that Goodness which, as we say, ' saves the soul ' with the relative values of the various good things that soothe or beautify life. For, if there is any value at all—I will not say in health and happiness, but in art, poetry, knowledge, refinement, public esteem, or human affection, and if their claims do clash, as in common opinion they sometimes do, with the demands of absolute sanctity, how is the balance to be struck? Are we to be content with the principle of accepting a little moral wrong for the sake of much material or artistic or intellectual advantage? That is the rule which the practical world follows, though without talking about it ; but the Stoics would have none of any such compromise.

Zeno first, like Antisthenes, denied any value whatever to these earthly things that are not virtue—to health or sickness, riches or poverty, beauty or ugliness, pain or pleasure ; who would ever mention them when the soul stood naked before God ? All that would then matter, and consequently all that can ever matter, is the goodness of the man's self, that is, of his free and living will. The Stoics improved on the military metaphor ; for to the soldier, after all, it does matter whether in his part of the field he wins or loses. Life is not like a battle but like a play, in which God has handed each man his part unread, and the good man proceeds to act it to the best of his power, not knowing what may happen in the last scene. He may become a crowned king, he may be a slave dying in torment. What matters it ? The good actor can play either part. All that matters is that he shall act his best, accept the order of the Cosmos and obey the Purpose of the great Dramaturge.

The answer seems absolute and unyielding, with no concession to the weakness of the flesh. Yet, in truth, it contains in itself the germ of a sublime practical compromise which makes Stoicism human. It accepts the Cosmos and it obeys the Purpose ; therefore there is a Cosmos, and there is a purpose in the world. Stoicism, like much of ancient thought at this period,

was permeated by the new discoveries of astronomy
and their formation into a coherent scientific system,
which remained unshaken till the days of Copernicus.
The stars, which had always moved men's wonder and
even worship, were now seen and proved to be no
wandering fires but parts of an immense and apparently
eternal order. One star might differ from another star
in glory, but they were all alike in their obedience to
law. They had their fixed courses, divine though they
were, which had been laid down for them by a Being
greater than they. The Order, or Cosmos, was a
proven fact ; therefore, the Purpose was a proven fact ;
and, though in its completeness inscrutable, it could at
least in part be divined from the fact that all these
varied and eternal splendours had for their centre our
Earth and its ephemeral master. The Purpose, though
it is not our Purpose, is especially concerned with us
and circles round us. It is the purpose of a God who
loves Man.

Let us forget that this system of astronomy has been
overthrown, and that we now know that Man is not
the centre of the universe. Let us forget that the
majestic order which reigns, or seems to reign, among
the stars, is matched by a brutal conflict and a chaos
of jarring purposes in the realms of those sciences which
deal with life.[1] If we can recover the imaginative

---

[1] e. g. the struggle for existence among animals and plants ; the
ἀλληλοφαγία, or 'mutual devouring', of animals ; and such points as
the various advances in evolution which seem self-destructive. Thus,
Man has learnt to stand on two feet and use his hands ; a great
advantage but one which has led to numerous diseases. Again,

outlook of the generations which stretched from, say, Meton in the fifth century before Christ to Copernicus in the sixteenth after, we shall be able to understand the spiritual exaltation with which men like Zeno or Poseidonius regarded the world.

We are part of an Order, a Cosmos, which we see to be infinitely above our comprehension but which we know to be an expression of love for Man ; what can we do but accept it, not with resignation but with enthusiasm, and offer to it with pride any sacrifice which it may demand of us. It is a glory to suffer for such an end.

And there is more. For the Stars show only what may be called a stationary purpose, an Order which is and remains for ever. But in the rest of the world, we can see a moving Purpose. It is Phusis, the word which the Romans unfortunately translated ' Natura ', but which means ' Growing ' or ' the way things grow '— almost what we call Evolution. But to the Stoic it is a living and conscious evolution, a forethought or Πρόνοια in the mind of God, what the Romans called *providentia*, guiding all things that grow in a direction which accords with the divine will. And the direction, the Stoic pointed out, was not towards mere happiness but towards *Aretê*, or the perfection of each thing or each species after its kind. *Phusis* shapes the acorn to grow into the perfect oak, the blind puppy into the good hound ; it makes the deer grow in swiftness to

physiologists say that the increasing size of the human head, especially when combined with the diminishing size of the pelvis, tends to make normal birth impossible.

perform the function of a deer, and man grow in power and wisdom to perform the function of a man. If a man is an artist it is his function to produce beauty; is he a governor, it is his function to produce a flourishing and virtuous city. True, the things that he produces are but shadows and in themselves utterly valueless; it matters not one straw whether the deer goes at ten miles an hour or twenty, whether the population of a city die this year of famine and sickness or twenty years hence of old age. But it belongs to the good governor to avert famine and to produce healthy conditions, as it belongs to the deer to run its best. So it is the part of a friend, if need arise, to give his comfort or his life for a friend; of a mother to love and defend her children; though it is true that in the light of eternity these ' creaturely ' affections shrivel into their native worthlessness. If the will of God is done, and done willingly, all is well. You may, if it brings you great suffering, feel the pain. You may even, through human weakness, weep or groan; that can be forgiven. Ἔσωθεν μέντοι μὴ στενάξῃς, ' But in the centre of your being groan not! ' Accept the Cosmos. Will joyously that which God wills and make the eternal Purpose your own.

I will say no more of this great body of teaching as I have dealt with it in a separate publication.[1] But I would point out two special advantages of a psychological kind which distinguish Stoicism from many

---

[1] *The Stoic Philosophy* (1915). See also Arnold's *Roman Stoicism* (1911); Bevan's *Stoics and Sceptics* (1913); and especially *Stoicorum Veterum Fragmenta* by von Arnim (1903–5).

systems of philosophy. First, though it never consciously faced the psychological problem of instinct, it did see clearly that man does not necessarily pursue what pleases him most, or what is most profitable to him, or even his ' good '. It saw that man can determine his end, and may well choose pain in preference to pleasure. This saved the school from a great deal of that false schematization which besets most forms of rationalistic psychology. Secondly, it did build up a system of thought on which, both in good days and evil, a life can be lived which is not only saintly, but practically wise and human and beneficent. It did for practical purposes solve the problem of living, without despair and without grave, or at least without gross, illusion.

The other great school of the fourth century, a school which, in the matter of ethics, may be called the only true rival of Stoicism, was also rooted in defeat. But it met defeat in a different spirit.[1] Epicurus, son of Neocles, of the old Athenian clan of the Philaïdae, was born on a colony in Samos in 341 B.C. His father was evidently poor ; else he would hardly have left Athens to live on a colonial farm, nor have had to eke out his farming by teaching an elementary school. We do not know how much the small boy learned from his father. But for older students there was a famous school on the

---

[1] The chief authorities on Epicurus are Usener's *Epicurea*, containing the *Life* from Diog. Laert., fragments and introduction : the papyrus fragments of Philodemus in *Volumina Herculanensia* ; Diogenes of Oenoanda (text by William, Teubner, 1907) ; the commentaries on Lucretius (Munro, Giussani, &c.).

neighbouring island of Teos, where a certain Nausiphanes taught the Ionian tradition of Mathematics and Physics as well as rhetoric and literary subjects. Epicurus went to this school when he was fourteen, and seems, among other things, to have imbibed the Atomic Theory of Democritus without realizing that it was anything peculiar. He felt afterwards as if his school-days had been merely a waste of time. At the age of eighteen he went to Athens, the centre of the philosophic world, but he only went, as Athenian citizens were in duty bound, to perform his year of military service as *ephêbus*. Study was to come later. The next year, however, 322, Perdiccas of Thrace made an attack on Samos and drove out the Athenian colonists. Neocles had by then lived on his bit of land for thirty years, and was old to begin life again. The ruined family took refuge in Colophon, and there Epicurus joined them. They were now too poor for the boy to go abroad to study philosophy. He could only make the best of a hard time and puzzle alone over the problems of life.

Recent years have taught us that there are few forms of misery harder than that endured by a family of refugees, and it is not likely to have been easier in ancient conditions. Epicurus built up his philosophy, it would seem, while helping his parents and brothers through this bad time. The problem was how to make the life of their little colony tolerable, and he somehow solved it. It was not the kind of problem which Stoicism and the great religions specially set themselves; it was at once too unpretending and too practical. One can easily imagine the condition for which he had to prescribe. For one thing, the unfortunate refugees all about him would torment themselves with unnecessary terrors. The Thracians were pursuing them. The Gods hated them ; they must obviously have committed some offence or impiety. (It is always easy for disheartened men to discover in themselves some sin that deserves punishment.) It would surely be better to die at once ; except that, with that sin upon them, they would only suffer more dreadfully beyond the grave ! In their distress they jarred, doubtless, on one another's nerves; and mutual bitterness doubled their miseries.

Epicurus is said to have had poor health, and the situation was one where even the best health would be sorely tried. But he had superhuman courage, and—what does not always go with such courage—a very affectionate and gentle nature. In later life all his three brothers were his devoted disciples—a testimonial accorded to few prophets or founders of religions. And he is the first man in the record of European history whose mother was an important element in his life. Some of his letters to her have been preserved, and show a touch of intimate affection which of course must have existed between human beings from the remotest times, but of which we possess no earlier record. And fragments of his letters to his friends strike the same note.[1]

[1] Epicurus is the one philosopher who protests with real indignation against that inhuman superiority to natural sorrows which is so much prized by most of the ancient schools. To him such ' apathy ' argues

His first discovery was that men torture themselves with unnecessary fears. He must teach them courage, θαρρεῖν ἀπὸ τῶν θεῶν, θαρρεῖν ἀπὸ ἀνθρώπων, to fear no evil from either man or God. God is a blessed being ; and no blessed being either suffers evil or inflicts evil on others. And as for men, most of the evils you fear from them can be avoided by Justice ; and if they do come, they can be borne. Death is like sleep, an unconscious state, nowise to be feared. Pain when it comes can be endured ; it is the anticipation that makes men miserable and saps their courage. The refugees were forgotten by the world, and had no hope of any great change in their condition. Well, he argued, so much the better ! Let them till the earth and love one another, and they would find that they had already in them that Natural Happiness which is man's possession until he throws it away. And of all things that contribute to happiness the greatest is Affection, φιλία.

Like the Cynics and Stoics, he rejected the world and all its conventions and prizes, its desires and passions and futility. But where the Stoic and Cynic proclaimed that in spite of all the pain and suffering of a wicked world, man can by the force of his own will be virtuous, Epicurus brought the more surprising good news that man can after all be happy.

either a hard heart or a morbid vanity (Fr. 120). His letters are full of affectionate expressions which rather shock the stern reserve of antique philosophy. He waits for one friend's ' heavenly presence ' (Fr. 165). He ' melts with a peculiar joy mingled with tears in remembering the last words ' of one who is dead (Fr. 186 ; cf. 213). He is enthusiastic about an act of kindness performed by another, who walked some five miles to help a barbarian prisoner (Fr. 194).

But to make this good news credible he had to construct a system of thought. He had to answer the temple authorities and their adherents among the vulgar, who threatened his followers with the torments of Hades for their impiety. He had to answer the Stoics and Cynics, preaching that all is worthless except Aretê; and the Sceptics, who dwelt on the fallibility of the senses, and the logical impossibility of knowledge.

He met the last of these by the traditional Ionian doctrine of sense-impressions, ingeniously developed. We can, he argued, know the outer world, because our sense impressions are literally ' impressions ' or stamps made by external objects upon our organs. To see, for instance, is to be struck by an infinitely tenuous stream of images, flowing from the object and directly imping- ing upon the retina. Such streams are flowing from all objects in every direction—an idea which seemed incredible until the modern discoveries about light, sound, and radiation. Thus there is direct contact with reality, and consequently knowledge. Besides direct vision, however, we have ' anticipations ', or προλήψεις, sometimes called ' common conceptions ', e. g. the general conception which we have of a horse when we are not seeing one. These are merely the result of repeated acts of vision. A curious result of this doctrine was that all our ' anticipations ' or ' common ideas ' are true; mistakes occur through some inter- pretation of our own which we add to the simple sensation.

We can know the world. How then are we to understand it? Here again Epicurus found refuge in the old Ionian theory of Atoms and the Void, which is supposed to have originated with Democritus and Leucippus, a century before. But Epicurus seems to have worked out the Atomic Theory more in detail, as we have it expounded in Lucretius' magnificent poem. In particular it was possibly he who first combined the Atomic Theory with hylozoism; i. e. he conceived of the Atoms as possessing some rudimentary power of movement and therefore able to swerve slightly in their regular downward course. That explains how they have become infinitely tangled and mingled, how plants and animals are alive, and how men have Free Will. It also enables Epicurus to build up a world without the assistance of a god. He set man free, as Lucretius says, from the ' burden of Religion ', though his doctrine of the ' blessed Being ' which neither has pain nor gives pain, enables him to elude the dangerous accusation of atheism. He can leave people believing in all their traditional gods, including even, if so they wish, ' the bearded Zeus and the helmed Athena ' which they see in dreams and in their ' common ideas ', while at the same time having no fear of them.

There remains the foolish fancy of the Cynics and Stoics that ' Aretê ' is the only good. Of course, he answers, Aretê is good; but that is because it produces happy life, or blessedness or pleasure or whatever you call it. He used normally the word ἡδονή ' sweetness ', and counted the Good as that which makes life sweet. He seems never to have entered into small disputes as to the difference between 'sweetness', or 'pleasure', and 'happiness' and 'well-being' (ἡδονή, εὐδαιμονία, εὐεστώ, κτλ.), though sometimes, instead of 'sweetness' he spoke of 'blessedness' (μακαριότης). Ultimately the dispute between him and the Stoics seems to resolve itself into a question whether the Good lies in πάσχειν or ποιεῖν, in Experience or in Action; and average human beings seem generally to think that the Good for a conscious being must be something of which he is conscious.

Thus the great system is built, simple, intelligible, dogmatic, and—as such systems go—remarkably water-tight. It enables man to be unafraid, and it helps him to be happy. The strange thing is that, although on more than one point it seems to anticipate most surprisingly the discoveries of modern science, it was accepted in a spirit more religious than scientific. As we can see from Lucretius it was taken almost as a revelation, from one who had saved mankind; whose intellect had pierced beyond the ' flaming walls of Heaven ' and brought back to man the gospel of an intelligible universe.[1]

---

[1] Lucretius, i. 62–79, actually speaks of the great atheist in language taken from the Saviour Religions (see below, p. 196):

> When Man's life upon earth in base dismay,
> Crushed by the burthen of Religion, lay,
> Whose face, from all the regions of the sky,
> Hung, glaring hate upon mortality,
> First one Greek man against her dared to raise
> His eyes, against her strive through all his days;
> Him noise of Gods nor lightnings nor the roar
> Of raging heaven subdued, but pricked the more

In 310 B. C., when Epicurus was thirty-two, things
had so far improved that he left Colophon and set up
a school of philosophy in Mytilene, but soon moved to
Lampsacus, on the Sea of Marmora, where he had
friends. Disciples gathered about him. Among them
were some of the leading men of the city, like Leonteus
and Idomeneus. The doctrine thrilled them and
seemed to bring freedom with it. They felt that such
a teacher must be set up in Athens, the home of the great
philosophers. They bought by subscription a house
and garden in Athens for 80 minae (about £320)[1] and
presented it to the Master. He crossed to Athens in
306 and, though he four times revisited Lampsacus
and has left letters addressed *To Friends in Lampsacus*,
he lived in the famous Garden for the rest of his life.

Friends from Lampsacus and elsewhere came and
lived with him or near him. The Garden was not only

> His spirit's valiance, till he longed the Gate
> To burst of this low prison of man's fate.
> And thus the living ardour of his mind
> Conquered, and clove its way ; he passed behind
> The world's last flaming wall, and through the whole
> Of space uncharted ranged his mind and soul.
> Whence, conquering, he returned to make Man see
> At last what can, what cannot, come to be ;
> By what law to each Thing its power hath been
> Assigned, and what deep boundary set between ;
> Till underfoot is tamed Religion trod,
> And, by His victory, Man ascends to God.

[1] That is, 8,000 drachmae. Rents had risen violently in 314 and so
presumably had land prices. Else one would say the Garden was about
the value of a good farm. See Tarn in *The Hellenistic Age* (1923),
p. 116.

a philosophical school ; it was also a sort of retreat or religious community. There lived there not only philosophers like Mêtrodôrus, Colôtes, Hermarchus, and others ; there were slaves, like Mys, and free women, like Themista, the wife of Leonteus, to both of whom the Master, as the extant fragments testify, wrote letters of intimate friendship. And not only free women, but women with names that show that they were slaves, Leontion, Nikidion, Mammarion. They were *hetairae*; perhaps victims of war, like many of the unfortunate heroines in the New Comedy ; free women from conquered cities, who had been sold in the slave market or reduced to misery as refugees, and to whom now the Garden afforded a true and spiritual refuge. For, almost as much as Diogenes, Epicurus had obliterated the stamp on the conventional currency. The values of the world no longer held good after you had passed the wicket gate of the Garden, and spoken with the Deliverer.

The Epicureans lived simply. They took neither flesh nor wine, and there is a letter extant, asking some one to send them a present of ' potted cheese '[1] as a special luxury. Their enemies, who were numerous and lively, make the obvious accusations about the hetairae, and cite an alleged letter of the Master to Leontion. ' Lord Paean, my dear little Leontion, your note fills me with such a bubble of excitement !'[2]

---

[1] τυρὸν κυθρίδιον, Fr. 182.

[2] Fr. 143. Παιὰν ἄναξ, φίλον Λεοντάριον, οἵου κροτοθορύβου ἡμᾶς ἀνέπλησας, ἀναγνόντας σου τὸ ἐπιστόλιον. Fr. 121 (from an enemy) implies that the Hetairae were expected to reform when they entered the Garden. Cf. Fr. 62 συνουσίη ὤνησε μὲν οὐδέποτε, ἀγαπητὸν δὲ εἰ μὴ ἔβλαψε : cf. Fr. 574.

The problem of this letter well illustrates the difficulty of forming clear judgements about the details of ancient life. Probably the letter is a forgery : we are definitely informed that there was a collection of such forgeries, made in order to damage Epicurus. But, if genuine, would it have seemed to a fair-minded contemporary a permissible or an impermissible letter for a philosopher to write ? By modern standards it would be about the border-line. And again, suppose it is a definite love-letter, what means have we of deciding whether Epicurus—or for that matter Zeno or Plato or any unconventional philosopher of this period— would have thought it blameworthy, or would merely have called our attention to the legal difficulties of contracting marriage with one who had been a Hetaira, and asked us how we expect men and women to live. Curiously enough, we happen to have the recorded sayings of Epicurus himself : ' The wise man will not fall in love ', and ' Physical union of the sexes never did good ; it is much if it does not do harm.'

This philosophy is often unjustly criticized. It is called selfish ; but that it is certainly not. It is always aiming at the deliverance of mankind [1] and it bases its happiness on φιλία, Friendship or Affection, just as the early Christians based it on ἀγάπη, a word no whit stronger than φιλία, though it is conventionally translated ' Love '. By this conception it becomes at once more human than the Stoa, to which, as to a Christian monk, human affection was merely a weakness of the flesh which might often conflict with the soul's duty

[1] See p. 204 below on Diogenes of Oenoanda.

towards God. Epicurus passionately protested against this unnatural ' apathy '. It was also human in that it recognized degrees of good or bad, of virtue or error. To the Stoic that which was not right was wrong. A calculator who says that seven sevens make forty-eight is just as wrong as one who says they make a thousand, and a sailor one inch below the surface of the water drowns just as surely as one who is a furlong deep. Just so in human life, wrong is wrong, falsehood is falsehood, and to talk of degrees is childish. Epicureanism had an easy and natural answer to these arguments, since pleasure and pain obviously admit of degrees.[1]

The school is blamed also for pursuing pleasure, on the ground that the direct pursuit of pleasure is self-defeating. But Epicurus never makes that mistake. He says that pleasure, or ' sweetness of life ', is the good ; but he never counsels the direct pursuit of it. Quite the reverse. He says that if you conquer your desires and fears, and live simply and love those about you, the natural sweetness of life will reveal itself.

A truer criticism is one which appears dimly in Plutarch and Cicero.[2] There is a strange shadow of sadness hanging over this wise and kindly faith, which proceeds from the essential distrust of life that lies at its heart. The best that Epicurus has really to say of the world is that if you are very wise and do not attract its notice—Λάθε βιώσας—it will not hurt you. It is

---

[1] Pleasures and pains may be greater or less, but the complete ' removal of pain and fear ' is a perfect end, not to be surpassed. Fr. 408-48, Ep. iii. 129-31.

[2] e. g. Plut. *Ne suaviter quidem vivi*, esp. chap. 17 (p. 1098 D).

a philosophy not of conquest but of escape. This was a weakness from which few of the fourth-century thinkers completely escaped. To aim at what we should call positive happiness was, to the Epicureans, only to court disappointment; better make it your aim to live without strong passion or desire, without high hopes or ambitions. Their professed ideals—παντὸς τοῦ ἀλγοῦντος ὑπεξαίρεσις, ἀταραξία, εὔροια, 'the removal of all active suffering', 'undisturbedness', 'a smooth flow'—seem to result in rather a low tension, in a life that is only half alive. We know that, as a matter of fact, this was not so. The Epicureans felt their doctrine to bring not mere comfort but inspiration and blessedness. The young Colotes, on first hearing the master speak, fell on his knees with tears and hailed him as a god.[1] We may compare the rapturous phrases of Lucretius. What can be the explanation of this?

Perhaps it is that a deep distrust of the world produces its own inward reaction, as starving men dream of rich banquets, and persecuted sects have apocalyptic visions of paradise. The hopes and desires that are starved of their natural sustenance project themselves on to some plane of the imagination. The martyr, even the most heretical martyr, sees the vision of his crown in the skies, the lover sees in obvious defects only rare and esoteric beauties. Epicurus avoided sedulously the transcendental optimism of the Stoics. He avoided mysticism, avoided allegory, avoided faith; he tried to set the feet of his philosophy on solid ground. He

[1] Cf. Fr. 141 when Epicurus writes to Colotes : 'Think of me as immortal, and go your ways as immortal too.'

can make a strong case for the probable happiness of a man of kindly affections and few desires, who asks little from the outside world. But after all it is only probable ; misfortunes and miseries may come to any man. ' Most of the evils you fear are false,' he answers, still reasonably. ' Death does not hurt. Poverty need never make a man less happy.' And actual pain ? ' Yes, pain may come. But you can endure it. Intense pains are brief ; long-drawn pains are not excruciating ; or seldom so.' Is that common-sense comfort not enough ? The doctrine becomes more intense both in its promises and its demands. If intense suffering comes, he enjoins, turn away your mind and conquer the pain by the ' sweetness ' of memory. There are in every wise man's life moments of intense beauty and delight ; if he has strength of mind he will call them back to him at will and live in the blessedness of the past, not in the mere dull agony of the moment. Nay, can he not actually enjoy the intellectual interest of this or that pang ? Has he not that within him which can make the quality of its own life ? On hearing of the death of a friend he will call back the sweetness of that friend's converse ; in the burning Bull of Phalaris he will think his thoughts and be glad. Illusion, the old Siren with whom man cannot live in peace, nor yet without her, has crept back unseen to the centre of the citadel. It was Epicurus, and not a Stoic or Cynic, who asserts that a Wise Man will be happy on the rack.[1]

Strangely obliging, ironic Fortune gave to him also

[1] Fr. 601 ; cf. 598 ff.

a chance of testing of his own doctrine. There is extant a letter written on his death-bed. ' I write to you on this blissful day which is the last of my life. The obstruction of my bladder and internal pains have reached the extreme point, but there is marshalled against them the delight of my mind in thinking over our talks together. Take care of the children of Metrodorus in a way worthy of your life-long devotion to me and to philosophy.' [1] At least his courage, and his kindness, did not fail.

Epicureanism had certainly its sublime side ; and from this very sublimity perhaps arose the greatest flaw in the system, regarded as a rational philosophy. It was accepted too much as a Revelation, too little as a mere step in the search for truth. It was based no doubt on careful and even profound scientific studies, and was expounded by the master in a vast array of volumes. But the result so attained was considered sufficient. Further research was not encouraged. Heterodoxy was condemned as something almost approaching ' parricide '.[2] The pursuit of ' needless knowledge ' was deliberately frowned upon.[3] When

---

[1] Fr. 138 ; cf. 177.

[2] ' οἱ τούτοις ἀντιγράφοντες οὐ πάνυ τι μακρὰν τῆς τῶν πατραλοιῶν καταδίκης ἀφεστήκασιν ', Fr. 49. Usener, from Philodemus, De Rhet. This may be only a playful reference to Plato's phrase about being a πατραλοίας of his father, Parmenides, Soph., p. 241 D.

[3] Epicurus congratulated himself (erroneously) that he came to Philosophy καθαρὸς πάσης παιδείας, ' undefiled by education '. Cf. Fr. 163 to Pythocles, παιδείαν δὲ πᾶσαν, μακάριε, φεῦγε τὸ ἀκάτιον ἀράμενος, ' From education in every shape, my son, spread sail and fly ! '

other philosophers were working out calculations about the size of the Sun and the commensurability of the sun-cycle and the moon-cycle, Epicurus contemptuously remarked that the Sun was probably about as big as it looked, or perhaps smaller; since fires at a distance generally look bigger than they are. The various theories of learned men were all possible but none certain. And as for the cycles, how did any one know that there was not a new sun shot off and extinguished every day ? [1] It is not surprising to find that none of the great discoveries of the Hellenistic Age were due to the Epicurean school. Lucretius, writing 250 years later, appears to vary hardly in any detail from the doctrines of the Master, and Diogenes of Oenoanda, 500 years later, actually repeats his letters and sayings word for word.

It is sad, this. It is un-Hellenic; it is a clear symptom of decadence from the free intellectual movement and the high hopes which had made the fifth century glorious. Only in one great school does the true Hellenic *Sôphrosynê* continue flourishing, a school whose modesty of pretension and quietness of language form a curious contrast with the rapt ecstasies of Stoic and Cynic and even, as we have seen, of Epicurean, just as its immense richness of scientific achievement contrasts with their comparative sterility. The Porch and the Garden offered new religions to raise from the dust men and women whose spirits were broken; Aristotle in his Open Walk, or *Peripatos*, brought philosophy and science and literature to guide the feet

[1] Fr. 343–6.

and interest the minds of those who still saw life steadily and tried their best to see it whole.

Aristotle was not lacking in religious insight and imagination, as he certainly was not without profound influence on the future history of religion. His complete rejection of mythology and of anthropomorphism; his resolute attempt to combine religion and science, not by sacrificing one to the other but by building the highest spiritual aspirations on ascertained truth and the probable conclusions to which it pointed; his splendid imaginative conception of the Divine Being or First Cause as unmoved itself while moving all the universe 'as the beloved moves the lover'; all these are high services to religious speculation, and justify the position he held, even when known only through a distorting Arabic translation, in medieval Christianity. If he had not written his other books he might well be famous now as a great religious teacher. But his theology is dwarfed by the magnificence and mass of his other work. And as a philosopher and man of science he does not belong to our present subject.

He is only mentioned here as a standard of that characteristic quality in Hellenism from which the rest of this book records a downfall. One variant of a well-known story tells how a certain philosopher, after frequenting the Peripatetic School, went to hear Chrysippus, the Stoic, and was transfixed. 'It was like turning from men to Gods.' It was really turning from Greeks to Semites, from philosophy to religion, from a school of very sober professions and high performance to one whose professions dazzled the reason.

'Come unto me,' cried the Stoic, 'all ye who are in storm or delusion ; I will show you the truth and the world will never grieve you more.'

Aristotle made no such profession. He merely thought and worked and taught better than other men. Aristotle is always surprising us not merely by the immense volume of clear thinking and co-ordinated knowledge of which he was master, but by the steady *Sôphrosynê* of his temper. Son of the court physician of Philip, tutor for some years to Alexander the Great, he never throughout his extant writings utters one syllable of flattery to his royal and world-conquering employers ; nor yet one syllable which suggests a grievance. He saw, at close quarters and from the winning side, the conquest of the Greek city states by the Macedonian *ethnos* or nation ; but he judges dispassionately that the city is the higher social form.

It seems characteristic that in his will, which is extant, after providing a dowry for his widow, Herpyllis, to facilitate her getting a second husband, and thanking her for her goodness to him, he directs that his bones are to be laid in the same grave with those of his first wife, Pythias, whom he had rescued from robbers more than twenty years before.[1]

Other philosophers disliked him because he wore no

---

[1] Pythias was the niece, or ward, of Aristotle's friend, Hermias, an extraordinary man who rose from slavery to be first a free man and a philosopher, and later Prince or 'Dynast' of Assos and Atarneus. In the end he was treacherously entrapped by the Persian General, Mentor, and crucified by the king. Aristotle's 'Ode to Virtue' is addressed to him. To his second wife, Herpyllis, Aristotle was only united by a civil marriage like the Roman *usus*.

long beard, dressed neatly and had good normal manners, and they despised his philosophy for very similar reasons. It was a school which took the existing world and tried to understand it instead of inventing some intense ecstatic doctrine which should transform it or reduce it to nothingness.

It possessed no Open Sesame to unlock the prison of mankind; yet it is not haunted by that *Oimôgê* of Kynoskephalai. While armies sweep Greece this way and that, while the old gods are vanquished and the cities lose their freedom and their meaning, the Peripatetics instead of passionately saving souls diligently pursued knowledge, and in generation after generation produced scientific results which put all their rivals into the shade.[1] In mathematics, astronomy, physics, botany, zoology, and biology, as well as the human sciences of literature and history, the Hellenistic Age was one of the most creative known to our record. And it is not only that among the savants responsible for these advances the proportion of Peripatetics is overwhelming; one may also notice that in this school alone it is assumed as natural that further research will take place and will probably correct as well as increase our knowledge, and that, when such corrections or differences of opinion do take place, there is no cry raised of Heresy.

It is the old difference between Philosophy and Religion, between the search of the intellect for truth and the cry of the heart for salvation. As the interest in truth for its own sake gradually abated in the ancient

---

[1] See note on Dicaearchus at end of chapter.

world, the works of Aristotle might still find com-
mentators, but his example was forgotten and his
influence confined to a small circle. The Porch and the
Garden, for the most part, divided between them the
allegiance of thoughtful men. Both systems had begun
in days of discomfiture, and aimed originally more at
providing a refuge for the soul than at ordering the
course of society. But after the turmoil of the fourth
century had subsided, when governments began again
to approach more nearly to peace and consequently to
justice, and public life once more to be attractive to
decent men, both philosophies showed themselves
adaptable to the needs of prosperity as well as adversity.
Many kings and great Roman governors professed
Stoicism. It held before them the ideal of universal
Brotherhood, and of duty to the ' Great Society of
Gods and Men ' ; it enabled them to work, indifferent
to mere pain and pleasure, as servants of the divine
purpose and ' fellow-workers with God ' in building up
a human Cosmos within the eternal Cosmos. It is
perhaps at first sight strange that many kings and
governors also followed Epicurus. Yet after all the
work of a public man is not hindered by a slight irony
as to the value of worldly greatness and a conviction
that a dinner of bread and water with love to season
it ' is better than all the crowns of the Greeks '. To
hate cruelty and superstition, to avoid passion and
luxury, to regard human ' pleasure ' or ' sweetness of
life ' as the goal to be aimed at, and ' friendship ' or
' kindliness ' as the principal element in that pleasure,
are by no means doctrines incompatible with wise and

effective administration. Both systems were good and both in a way complementary one to another. They still divide between them the practical philosophy of western mankind. At times to most of us it seems as though nothing in life had value except to do right and to fear not; at others that the only true aim is to make mankind happy. At times man's best hope seems to lie in that part of him which is prepared to defy or condemn the world of fact if it diverges from the ideal; in that intensity of reverence which will accept many impossibilities rather than ever reject a holy thing; above all in that uncompromising moral sensitiveness to which not merely the corruptions of society but the fundamental and necessary facts of animal existence seem both nauseous and wicked, links and chains in a system which can never be the true home of the human spirit. At other times men feel the need to adapt their beliefs and actions to the world as it is; to brush themselves free from cobwebs; to face plain facts with common sense and as much kindliness as life permits, meeting the ordinary needs of a perishable and imperfect species without illusion and without make-believe. At one time we are Stoics, at another Epicureans.

But amid their differences there is one faith which was held by both schools in common. It is the great characteristic faith of the ancient world, revealing itself in many divergent guises and seldom fully intelligible to modern men; faith in the absolute supremacy of the inward life over things external. These men really believed that wisdom is more precious than jewels, that poverty and ill health are things of no import, that the good man is happy whatever befall him, and all the rest. And in generation after generation many of the ablest men, and women also, acted upon the belief. They lived by free choice lives whose simplicity and privation would horrify a modern labourer, and the world about them seems to have respected rather than despised their poverty. To the Middle Age, with its monks and mendicants expectant of reward in heaven, such an attitude, except for its disinterestedness, would be easily understood. To some eastern nations, with their cults of asceticism and contemplation, the same doctrines have appealed almost like a physical passion or a dangerous drug running riot in their veins. But modern western man cannot believe them, nor believe seriously that others believe them. On us the power of the material world has, through our very mastery of it and the dependence which results from that mastery, both inwardly and outwardly increased its hold. *Capta ferum victorem cepit.* We have taken possession of it, and now we cannot move without it.

The material element in modern life is far greater than in ancient; but it does not follow that the spiritual element is correspondingly less. No doubt it is true that a naval officer in a conning-tower in a modern battle does not need less courage and character than a naked savage who meets his enemy with a stick and a spear. Yet probably in the first case the battle is mainly decided by the weight and accuracy of the guns, in the second by the qualities of the fighter. Consequently the modern world thinks more incessantly and anxiously about the guns, that is, about money and mechanism; the ancient devotes its thought more to human character and duty. And it is curious to observe how, in general, each tries to remedy what is wrong with the world by the method that is habitually in its thoughts. Speaking broadly, apart from certain religious movements, the enlightened modern reformer, if confronted with some ordinary complex of misery and wickedness, instinctively proposes to cure it by higher wages, better food, more comfort and leisure; to make people comfortable and trust to their becoming good. The typical ancient reformer would appeal to us to care for none of those things (since riches notoriously do not make men virtuous), but with all our powers to pursue wisdom or righteousness and the life of the spirit; to be good men, as we can be if we will, and to know that all else will follow.

This is one of the regions in which the ancients might have learned much from us, and in which we still have much to learn from them, if once we can shake off our temporal obsessions and listen.

NOTE

As an example it is worth noticing, even in a bare catalogue, the work done by one of Aristotle's own pupils, a Peripatetic of the second rank, Dicaearchus of Messene. His *floruit* is given as 310 B.C. Dorian by birth, when Theophrastus was made head of the school he retired to the Peloponnese, and shows a certain prejudice against Athens.

One of the discoveries of the time was biography. And, by a

brilliant stroke of imagination Dicaearchus termed one of his books Βίος Ἑλλάδος, *The Life of Hellas*. He saw civilization as the biography of the world. First, the Age of Cronos, when man as a simple savage made no effort after higher things; next, the ancient river-civilizations of the orient; third, the Hellenic system. Among his scanty fragments we find notes on such ideas as πάτρα, φρατρία, φυλή, as Greek institutions. The *Life of Hellas* was much used by late writers. It formed the model for another Βίος Ἑλλάδος by a certain Jason, and for Varro's *Vita Populi Romani*.

Then, like his great master, Dicaearchus made studies of the Constitutions of various states (e. g. Pellene, Athens, and Corinth); his treatise on the Constitution of Sparta was read aloud annually in that city by order of the Ephors. It was evidently appreciative.

A more speculative work was his *Tripoliticus*, arguing that the best constitution ought to be compounded of the three species, monarchic, aristocratic, and democratic, as in Sparta. Only then would it be sure to last. Polybius accepted the principle of the Mixed Constitution, but found his ideal in the constitution of Rome, which later history was to prove so violently unstable. Cicero, *De Republica*, takes the same line (Polyb. vi. 2–10; Cic. *De Rep.* i. 45; ii. 65). Dicaearchus treated of similar political subjects in his public addresses at Olympia and at the Panathenaea.

We hear more about his work on the history of literature, though his generation was almost the first to realize that such a subject had any existence. He wrote *Lives of Philosophers*—a subject hitherto not considered worth recording—giving the biographical facts followed by philosophic and aesthetic criticism. We hear, for example, of his life of Plato; of Pythagoras (in which he laid emphasis on the philosopher's practical work), of Xenophanes, and of the Seven Wise Men.

He also wrote *Lives of Poets*. We hear of books on Alcaeus and on Homer, in which latter he is said to have made the startling remark that the poems ' should be pronounced in the Aeolic dialect '. Whatever this remark exactly meant, and we cannot tell without the context, it seems an extraordinary anticipation of modern philological discoveries. He wrote on the *Hypotheses*—i. e. the subject matter—*of Sophocles and Euripides*; also on *Musical Contests*, περὶ Μουσικῶν ἀγώνων, carrying further Aristotle's own collection of the *Didascaliae*, or official notices of the production of Tragedies in Athens. The book dealt both with dates and with customs; it told how Skolia were sung, with a laurel or myrtle twig in the hand, how Sophocles introduced a third actor, and the like.

In philosophy proper he wrote On the Soul, περὶ ψυχῆς. His first book, the *Corinthiacus*, proved that the Soul was a 'harmony' or 'right blending' of the four elements, and was identical with the force of the living body. The second, the *Lesbiacus*, drew the conclusion that, if a compound, it was destructible. (Hence a great controversy with his master.)

He wrote περὶ φθορᾶς ἀνθρώπων, on the *Perishing of Mankind*; i.e. on the way in which large masses of men have perished off the earth, through famine, pestilence, wild beasts, war, and the like. He decides that Man's most destructive enemy is Man. (The subject may have been suggested to him by a fine imaginative passage in Aristotle's *Meteorology* (i. 14, 7) dealing with the vast changes that have taken place on the earth's surface and the unrecorded perishings of races and communities.)

He wrote a treatise against *Divination*, and a (satirical ?) *Descent to the Cave of Trophonius*. He seems, however, to have allowed some importance to dreams and to the phenomena of 'possession'.

And, with all this, we have not touched on his greatest work, which was in the sphere of geography. He wrote a Περίοδος γῆς, a *Journey Round the Earth*, accompanied with a map. He used for this map the greatly increased stores of knowledge gained by the Macedonian expeditions over all Asia as far as the Ganges. He also seems to have devised the method of denoting the position of a place by means of two co-ordinates, the method soon after developed by Eratosthenes into Latitude and Longitude. He attempted calculations of the measurements of large geographical distances, for which of course both his data and his instruments were inadequate. Nevertheless his measurements remained a well-known standard; we find them quoted and criticized by Strabo and Polybius. And, lastly, he published *Measurements of the Heights of Mountains in the Peloponnese*; but the title seems to have been unduly modest, for we find in the fragments statements about mountains far outside that area; about Pelion and

Olympus in Thessaly and of Atabyrion in Rhodes. He had a sub-vention, Pliny tells us (N. H. ii. 162, ' regum cura permensus montes '), from the king of Macedon, probably either Cassander or, as one would like to believe, the philosophic Antigonus Gonatas. And he calculated the heights, so we are told, by trigonometry, using the δίοπτρα, an instrument of hollow reeds without lenses which served for his primitive theodolite. It is an extraordinary record, and illustrates the true Peripatetic spirit.

IV

THE FAILURE OF NERVE

IV

THE FAILURE OF NERVE

ANY one who turns from the great writers of classical Athens, say Sophocles or Aristotle, to those of the Christian era must be conscious of a great difference in tone. There is a change in the whole relation of the writer to the world about him. The new quality is not specifically Christian : it is just as marked in the Gnostics and Mithras-worshippers as in the Gospels and the Apocalypse, in Julian and Plotinus as in Gregory and Jerome. It is hard to describe. It is a rise of asceticism, of mysticism, in a sense, of pessimism ; a loss of self-confidence, of hope in this life and of faith in normal human effort ; a despair of patient inquiry, a cry for infallible revelation ; an indifference to the welfare of the state, a conversion of the soul to God. It is an atmosphere in which the aim of the good man is not so much to live justly, to help the society to which he belongs and enjoy the esteem of his fellow creatures ; but rather, by means of a burning faith, by contempt for the world and its standards, by ecstasy, suffering, and martyrdom, to be granted pardon for his unspeakable unworthiness, his immeasurable sins. There is an intensifying of certain spiritual emotions ; an increase of sensitiveness, a failure of nerve.

Now this antithesis is often exaggerated by the

admirers of one side or the other. A hundred people write as if Sophocles had no mysticism and practically speaking no conscience. Half a dozen retort as if St. Paul had no public spirit and no common sense. I have protested often against this exaggeration ; but, stated reasonably, as a change of proportion and not a creation of new hearts, the antithesis is certainly based on fact. The historical reasons for it are suggested above, in the first of these essays.

My description of this complicated change is, of course, inadequate, but not, I hope, one-sided. I do not depreciate the religions that followed on this movement by describing the movement itself as a 'failure of nerve'. Mankind has not yet decided which of two opposite methods leads to the fuller and deeper knowledge of the world : the patient and sympathetic study of the good citizen who lives in it, or the ecstatic vision of the saint who rejects it. But probably most Christians are inclined to believe that without some failure and sense of failure, without a contrite heart and conviction of sin, man can hardly attain the religious life. I can imagine an historian of this temper believing that the period we are about to discuss was a necessary softening of human pride, a *Praeparatio Evangelica*.[1]

---

[1] Mr. Marett has pointed out that this conception has its roots deep in primitive human nature : *The Birth of Humility*, Oxford, 1910, p. 17. ' It would, perhaps, be fanciful to say that man tends to run away from the sacred as uncanny, to cower before it as secret, and to prostrate himself before it as tabu. On the other hand, it seems plain that to these three negative qualities of the sacred taken together there corresponds on the part of man a certain negative attitude of

I am concerned in this paper with the lower country lying between two great ranges. The one range is Greek Philosophy, culminating in Plato, Aristotle, the Porch, and the Garden ; the other is Christianity, culminating in St. Paul and his successors. The one is the work of Hellas, using some few foreign elements ; the second is the work of Hellenistic culture on a Hebrew stock. The books of Christianity are Greek, the philosophical background is Hellenistic, the result of the interplay, in the free atmosphere of Greek philosophy, of religious ideas derived from Egypt, Anatolia, Syria, and Babylon. The preaching is carried on in Greek among the Greek-speaking workmen of the great manufacturing and commercial cities. The first preachers are Jews : the central scene is set in Jerusalem. I wish in this essay to indicate how

---

mind. Psychologists class the feelings bound up with flight, cowering, and prostration under the common head of " asthenic emotion ". In plain English they are all forms of heart-sinking, of feeling unstrung. This general type of innate disposition would seem to be the psychological basis of Humility. Taken in its social setting, the emotion will, of course, show endless shades of complexity ; for it will be excited, and again will find practical expression, in all sorts of ways. Under these varying conditions, however, it is reasonable to suppose that what Mr. McDougall would call the " central part " of the experience remains very much the same. In face of the sacred the normal man is visited by a heart-sinking, a wave of asthenic emotion.' Mr. Marett continues : ' If that were all, however, Religion would be a matter of pure fear. But it is not all. There is yet the positive side of the sacred to be taken into account.' It is worth remarking also that Schleiermacher (1767-1834) placed the essence of religion in the feeling of absolute dependence without attempting to define the object towards which it was directed.

a period of religious history, which seems broken, is really continuous, and to trace the lie of the main valleys which lead from the one range to the other, through a large and imperfectly explored territory.

The territory in question is the so-called Hellenistic Age, the period during which the Schools of Greece were 'hellenizing' the world. It is a time of great enlightenment, of vigorous propaganda, of high importance to history. It is a time full of great names : in one school of philosophy alone we have Zeno, Cleanthes, Chrysippus, Panaetius, Posidonius. Yet, curiously enough, it is represented in our tradition by something very like a mere void. There are practically no complete books preserved, only fragments and indirect quotations. Consequently in the search for information about this age we must throw our nets wide. Beside books and inscriptions of the Hellenistic period proper I have drawn on Cicero, Pliny, Seneca, and the like for evidence about their teachers and masters. I have used many Christian and Gnostic documents and works like the Corpus of Hermetic writings and the Mithras Liturgy. Among modern writers I must acknowledge a special debt to the researches of Dieterich, Cumont, Bousset, Wendland, and Reitzenstein.

The Hellenistic Age seems at first sight to have entered on an inheritance such as our speculative Anarchists sometimes long for, a *tabula rasa*, on which a new and highly gifted generation of thinkers might write clean and certain the book of their discoveries about life—what Herodotus would call their '*Historiê*'.

For, as we have seen in the last essay, it is clear that by
the time of Plato the traditional religion of the Greek
states was, if taken at its face value, a bankrupt concern.
There was hardly one aspect in which it could bear
criticism ; and in the kind of test that chiefly matters,
the satisfaction of men's ethical requirements and
aspirations, it was if anything weaker than elsewhere.
Now a religious belief that is scientifically preposterous
may still have a long and comfortable life before it.
Any worshipper can suspend the scientific part of his
mind while worshipping. But a religious belief that
is morally contemptible is in serious danger, because
when the religious emotions surge up the moral
emotions are not far away. And the clash cannot be
hidden.

This collapse of the traditional religion of Greece
might not have mattered so much if the form of Greek
social life had remained. If a good Greek had his
Polis, he had an adequate substitute in most respects
for any mythological gods. But the Polis too, as we
have seen in the last essay, fell with the rise of Macedon.
It fell, perhaps, not from any special spiritual fault of
its own ; it had few faults except its fatal narrowness ;
but simply because there now existed another social
whole, which, whether higher or lower in civilization,
was at any rate utterly superior in brute force and in
money. Devotion to the Polis lost its reality when the
Polis, with all that it represented of rights and laws and
ideals of Life, lay at the mercy of a military despot, who
might, of course, be a hero, but might equally well be
a vulgar sot or a corrupt adventurer.

What the succeeding ages built upon the ruins of the Polis is not our immediate concern. In the realm of thought, on the whole, the Polis triumphed. Aristotle based his social theory on the Polis, not the nation. Dicaearchus, Didymus, and Posidonius followed him, and we still use his language. Rome herself was a Polis, as well as an Empire. And Professor Haverfield has pointed out that a City has more chance of taking in the whole world to its freedoms and privileges than a Nation has of making men of alien birth its compatriots. A Jew of Tarsus could easily be granted the civic rights of Rome : he could never have been made an Italian or a Frenchman. The Stoic ideal of the World as ' one great City of Gods and Men ' has not been surpassed by any ideal based on the Nation.

What we have to consider is the general trend of religious thought from, say, the Peripatetics to the Gnostics. It is a fairly clear history. A soil once teeming with wild weeds was to all appearance swept bare and made ready for new sowing : skilled gardeners chose carefully the best of herbs and plants and tended the garden sedulously. But the bounds of the garden kept spreading all the while into strange untended ground, and even within the original walls the weeding had been hasty and incomplete. At the end of a few generations all was a wilderness of weeds again, weeds rank and luxuriant and sometimes extremely beautiful, with a half-strangled garden flower or two gleaming here and there in the tangle of them. Does that comparison seem disrespectful to religion ? Is philosophy all flowers and traditional belief all weeds ? Well, think what a weed is. It is only a name for all the natural wild vegetation which the earth sends up of herself, which lives and will live without the conscious labour of man. The flowers are what we keep alive with difficulty ; the weeds are what conquer us.

It has been well observed by Zeller that the great weakness of all ancient thought, not excepting Socratic thought, was that instead of appealing to objective experiment it appealed to some subjective sense of fitness. There were exceptions, of course : Democritus, Eratosthenes, Hippocrates, and to a great extent Aristotle. But in general there was a strong tendency to follow Plato in supposing that people could really solve questions by an appeal to their inner consciousness. One result of this, no doubt, was a tendency to lay too much stress on mere agreement. It is obvious, when one thinks about it, that quite often a large number of people who know nothing about a subject will all agree and all be wrong. Yet we find the most radical of ancient philosophers unconsciously dominated by the argument *ex consensu gentium*. It is hard to find two more uncompromising thinkers than Zeno and Epicurus. Yet both of them, when they are almost free from the popular superstitions, when they have constructed complete systems which, if not absolutely logic-proof, are calculated at least to keep out the weather for a century or so, open curious side-doors at the last moment and let in all the gods of mythology.[1] True, they are admitted as

---

[1] Usener, *Epicurea* (1887), pp. 232 ff. ; Diels, *Doxographi Graeci* (1879), p. 306 ; Arnim, *Stoicorum Veterum Fragmenta* (1903–5), Chrysippus 1014, 1019.

suspicious characters, and under promise of good behaviour. Epicurus explains that they do not and cannot do anything whatever to anybody; Zeno explains that they are not anthropomorphic, and are only symbols or emanations or subordinates of the all-ruling Unity; both parties get rid of the myths. But the two great reformers have admitted a dangerous principle. The general consensus of humanity, they say, shows that there are gods, and gods which in mind, if not also in visual appearance, resemble man. Epicurus succeeded in barring the door, and admitted nothing more. But the Stoics presently found themselves admitting or insisting that the same consensus proved the existence of daemons, of witchcraft, of divination, and when they combined with the Platonic school, of more dangerous elements still.

I take the Stoics and Epicureans as the two most radical schools. On the whole both of them fought steadily and strongly against the growth of superstition, or, if you like to put it in other language, against the dumb demands of man's infra-rational nature. The glory of the Stoics is to have built up a religion of extraordinary nobleness; the glory of the Epicureans is to have upheld an ideal of sanity and humanity stark upright amid a reeling world, and, like the old Spartans, never to have yielded one inch of ground to the common foe.

The great thing to remember is that the mind of man cannot be enlightened permanently by merely teaching him to reject some particular set of super-stitions. There is an infinite supply of other super-

stitions always at hand; and the mind that desires
such things—that is, the mind that has not trained
itself to the hard discipline of reasonableness and
honesty, will, as soon as its devils are cast out, proceed
to fill itself with their relations.

Let us first consider the result of the mere denial
of the Olympian religion. The essential postulate of
that religion was that the world is governed by a
number of definite personal gods, possessed of a human
sense of justice and fairness and capable of being influenced by normal human motives. In general, they
helped the good and punished the bad, though doubtless they tended too much to regard as good those who
paid them proper attention and as bad those who did
not.

Speaking broadly, what was left when this conception proved inadequate? If it was not these personal
gods who made things happen, what was it? If the
Tower of Siloam was not deliberately thrown down
by the gods so as to kill and hurt a carefully collected
number of wicked people, while letting the good
escape, what was the explanation of its falling? The
answer is obvious, but it can be put in two ways. You
can either say : ' It was just chance that the Tower
fell at that particular moment when So-and-so was
under it.' Or you can say, with rather more reflection
but not any more common sense : ' It fell because of
a definite chain of causes, a certain degree of progressive
decay in the building, a certain definite pressure, &c.
It was bound to fall.'

There is no real difference in these statements, at least in the meaning of those who ordinarily utter them. Both are compatible with a reasonable and scientific view of the world. But in the Hellenistic Age, when Greek thought was spreading rapidly and superficially over vast semi-barbarous populations whose minds were not ripe for it, both views turned back instinctively into a theology as personal as that of the Olympians. It was not, of course, Zeus or Apollo who willed this ; every one knew so much : it happened by Chance. That is, Chance or Fortune willed it. And Τύχη became a goddess like the rest. The great catastrophes, the great transformations of the mediterranean world which marked the Hellenistic period, had a strong influence here. If Alexander and his generals had practised some severely orthodox Macedonian religion, it would have been easy to see that the Gods of Macedon were the real rulers of the world. But they most markedly did not. They accepted hospitably all the religions that crossed their path. Some power or other was disturbing the world, that was clear. It was not exactly the work of man, because sometimes the good were exalted, sometimes the bad ; there was no consistent purpose in the story. It was just Fortune. Happy is the man who knows how to placate Fortune and make her smile upon him !

It is worth remembering that the best seed-ground for superstition is a society in which the fortunes of men seem to bear practically no relation to their merits and efforts. A stable and well-governed society does tend, speaking roughly, to ensure that the Virtuous

and Industrious Apprentice shall succeed in life, while
the Wicked and Idle Apprentice fails. And in such
a society people tend to lay stress on the reasonable
or visible chains of causation. But in a country
suffering from earthquakes or pestilences, in a court
governed by the whim of a despot, in a district which
is habitually the seat of a war between alien armies,
the ordinary virtues of diligence, honesty, and kindliness seem to be of little avail. The only way to escape
destruction is to win the favour of the prevailing
powers, take the side of the strongest invader, flatter
the despot, placate the Fate or Fortune or angry
god that is sending the earthquake or the pestilence.
The Hellenistic period pretty certainly falls in some
degree under all of these categories. And one result is
the sudden and enormous spread of the worship of
Fortune. Of course, there was always a protest.
There is the famous

> *Nullum numen habes si sit prudentia : nos te,*
> *Nos facimus, Fortuna, deam,*

taken by Juvenal from the Greek. There are many
unguarded phrases and at least three corrections in
Polybius.[1] Most interesting of all perhaps, there is the
first oration of Plutarch on the Fortune of Alexander.[2]

---

[1] Juv. x. 365 f. ; Polyb. ii. 38, 5 ; x. 5, 8 ; xviii. 11, 5.

[2] Cf. also his *Consolatio ad Apollonium.* The earliest text is
perhaps the interesting fragment of Demetrius of Phalerum (fr. 19,
in *F. H. G.* ii. 368), written about 317 B. C. It is quoted with admiration by Polybius xxix. 21, with reference to the defeat of Perseus of
Macedon by the Romans :

' One must often remember the saying of Demetrius of Phalerum . . .

A sentence in Pliny's *Natural History*, ii. 22, seems to go back to Hellenistic sources :

' Throughout the whole world, at every place and hour, by every voice Fortune alone is invoked and her name spoken : she is the one defendant, the one culprit, the one thought in men's minds, the one object of praise, the one cause. She is worshipped with insults, counted as fickle and often as blind, wandering, inconsistent, elusive, changeful, and friend of the unworthy. . . . We are so much at the mercy of chance that Chance is our god.'

The word used is first *Fortuna* and then *Sors*. This shows how little real difference there is between the two apparently contradictory conceptions.—' Chance would have it so.' ' It was fated to be.' The sting of both phrases—their pleasant bitterness when played

in his Treatise on Fortune. . . . "If you were to take not an indefinite time, nor many generations, but just the fifty years before this, you could see in them the violence of Fortune. Fifty years ago do you suppose that either the Macedonians or the King of Macedon, or the Persians or the King of Persia, if some God had foretold them what was to come, would ever have believed that by the present time the Persians, who were then masters of almost all the inhabited world, would have ceased to be even a geographical name, while the Macedonians, who were then not even a name, would be rulers of all ? Yet this Fortune, who bears no relation to our method of life, but transforms everything in the way we do not expect and displays her power by surprises, is at the present moment showing all the world that, when she puts the Macedonians into the rich inheritance of the Persian, she has only lent them these good things until she changes her mind about them." Which has now happened in the case of Perseus. The words of Demetrius were a prophecy uttered, as it were, by inspired lips.'

with, their quality of poison when believed—lies in
their denial of the value of human endeavour.

Yet on the whole, as one might expect, the believers
in Destiny are a more respectable congregation than
the worshippers of Chance.   It requires a certain
amount of thoughtfulness to rise to the conception that
nothing really happens without a cause. It is the beginning, perhaps, of science. Ionic philosophers of the fifth
century had laid stress on the Ἀνάγκη φύσιος,[1] what
we should call the Chain of causes in Nature. After the
rise of Stoicism Fate becomes something less physical,
more related to conscious purpose.   It is not *Ananke*
but *Heimarmene*. Heimarmene, in the striking simile
of Zeno,[2] is like a fine thread running through the whole
of existence—the world, we must remember, was to
the Stoics a live thing—like that invisible thread of life
which, in heredity, passes on from generation to generation of living species and keeps the type alive ; it runs
causing, causing for ever, both the infinitesimal and
the infinite.   It is the Λόγος τοῦ Κόσμου,[3] the Νοῦς Διός,
the Reason of the World or the mind of Zeus, rather
difficult to distinguish from the Pronoia or Providence
which is the work of God and indeed the very essence
of God.   Thus it is not really an external and alien
force.   For the human soul itself is a fragment or
effluence of the divine, and this Law of God is also the
law of man's own Phusis. As long as you act in accordance with your true self you are complying with that

---

[1] Eur., *Tro.* 886. Literally it means ' The Compulsion in the way
Things grow '.

[2] Zeno, fr. 87, Arnim.   [3] Chrysippus, fr. 913, Arnim.

divine Εἱμαρμένη or Πρόνοια, whose service is perfect
freedom. Only when you are false to your own nature
and become a rebel against the kingdom of God which
is within you, are you dragged perforce behind the
chariot-wheels. The doctrine is implied in Cleanthes'
celebrated Hymn to Destiny and is explained clearly
by Plotinus.[1]

That is a noble conception. But the vulgar of course
can turn Kismet into a stupid idol, as easily as they can
Fortune. And Epicurus may have had some excuse
for exclaiming that he would sooner be a slave to the
old gods of the vulgar, than to the Destiny of the
philosophers.[2]

So much for the result in superstitious minds of the
denial, or rather the removal, of the Olympian Gods.
It landed men in the worship of Fortune or of Fate.

Next, let us consider what happened when, instead
of merely rejecting the Gods *en masse*, people tried
carefully to collect what remained of religion after
the Olympian system fell.

Aristotle himself gives us a fairly clear answer. He
held that the origins of man's idea (ἔννοια) of the
Divine were twofold,[3] the phenomena of the sky and
the phenomena of the human soul. It is very much
what Kant found two thousand years later. The
spectacle of the vast and ordered movements of the

---

[1] Cleanthes, 527, Arnim. Ἄγου δέ μ', ὦ Ζεῦ, καὶ σύ γ' ἡ Πεπρω-
μένη, κτλ. Plotinus, *Enn.* III. i. 10.

[2] Epicurus, Third Letter. Usener, p. 65, 12 = Diog. La. x. 134.

[3] Aristotle, fr. 12 ff.

heavenly bodies are compared by him in a famous fragment with the marching forth of Homer's armies before Troy. Behind such various order and strength there must surely be a conscious mind capable

Κοσμῆσαι ἵππους τε καὶ ἀνέρας ἀσπιδιώτας,
To order steeds of war and mailèd men.

It is only a step from this to regarding the sun, moon, and stars as themselves divine, and it is a step which both Plato and Aristotle, following Pythagoras and followed by the Stoics, take with confidence. Chrysippus gives practically the same list of gods : ' the Sun, Moon, and Stars; and Law: and men who have become Gods.' [1] Both the wandering stars and the fixed stars are ' animate beings, divine and eternal ', self-acting subordinate gods. As to the divinity of the soul or the mind of man, the earlier generations are shy about it. But in the later Stoics it is itself a portion of the divine life. It shows this ordinarily by its power of reason, and more conspicuously by becoming ἔνθεος, or ' filled with God ', in its exalted moments of pre-vision, ecstasy, and prophetic dreams. If reason itself is divine, there is something else in the soul which is even higher than reason or at least more surprisingly divine.

Let us follow the history of both these remaining substitutes for the Olympian gods.

First for the Heavenly bodies. If they are to be made divine, we can hardly stop there. The Earth is also a divine being. Old tradition has always said

---

[1] e. g. Chrysippus, fr. 1076, Arnim.

so, and Plato has repeated it. And if Earth is divine, so surely are the other elements, the *Stoicheia*, Water, Air, and above all, Fire. For the Gods themselves are said by Plato to be made of fire, and the Stars visibly are so. Though perhaps the heavenly Fire is really not our Fire at all, but a πέμπτον σῶμα, a 'Fifth Body', seeing that it seems not to burn nor the Stars to be consumed.

This is persuasive enough and philosophic; but whither has it led us? Back to the Olympians, or rather behind the Olympians; as St. Paul puts it (Gal. iv. 9), to 'the beggarly elements'. The old Korê, or Earth Maiden and Mother, seems to have held her own unshaken by the changes of time all over the Aegean area. She is there in prehistoric Crete with her two lions; with the same lions orientalized in Olympia and Ephesus; in Sparta with her great marsh birds; in Boeotia with her horse. She runs riot in a number of the Gnostic systems both pre-Christian and post-Christian. She forms a divine triad with the Father and the Son: that is ancient and natural. But she also becomes the Divine Wisdom, Sophia, the Divine Truth, Aletheia, the Holy Breath or Spirit, the Pneuma. Since the word for 'spirit' is neuter in Greek and masculine in Latin, this last is rather a surprise. It is explained when we remember that in Hebrew the word for Spirit, 'Ruah', is mostly feminine. In the meantime let us notice one curious development in the life of this goddess. In the old religion of Greece and Western Asia, she begins as a Maiden, then in fullness of time becomes a mother. There is evidence also for a third stage, the widowhood of withering autumn.[1]   To the classical Greek this motherhood was quite as it should be, a due fulfilment of normal functions.   But to the Gnostic and his kind it connoted a ' fall ', a passage from the glory of Virginity to a state of Sin.[2]   The Korê becomes a fallen Virgin, sometimes a temptress or even a female devil ; sometimes she has to be saved by her Son the Redeemer.[3]   As far as I have observed, she loses most of her earthly agricultural quality, though as Selene or even Helen she keeps up her affinity with the Moon.

Almost all the writers of the Hellenistic Age agree in regarding the Sun, Moon, and Stars as gods.   The rationalists Hecataeus and Euhemerus, before going on to their deified men, always start with the heavenly bodies.   When Plutarch explains in his beautiful and kindly way that all religions are really attempts towards the same goal, he clinches his argument by observing that we all see the same Sun and Moon though we call them by different names in all languages.[4]   But the belief does not seem to have had much religious

---

[1] *Themis*, p. 180, n. 1.

[2] Not to Plotinus : *Enn.* ii. ix against the Valentinians.   Cf. Porphyry, 'Αφορμαί, 28.

[3] Bousset, *Hauptprobleme der Gnosis*, 1907, pp. 13, 21, 26, 81, &c. ; pp. 332 ff.   She becomes Helen in the beautiful myth of the Simonian Gnostics—a Helen who has forgotten her name and race, and is a slave in a brothel in Tyre.   Simon discovers her, gradually brings back her memory and redeems her.   Irenaeus, i. 23, 2.

[4] *De Iside et Osiride*, 67.   (He distinguishes them from the real God, however, just as Sallustius would.)

intensity in it, until it was reinforced by two alien influences.

First, we have the ancient worship of the Sun, implicit, if not explicit, in a great part of the oldest Greek rituals, and then idealized by Plato in the *Republic*, where the Sun is the author of all light and life in the material world, as the Idea of Good is in the ideal world. This worship came gradually into contact with the traditional and definite Sun-worship of Persia. The final combination took place curiously late. It was the Roman conquests of Cilicia, Cappadocia, Commagene, and Armenia that gave the decisive moment.[1] To men who had wearied of the myths of the poets, who could draw no more inspiration from their Apollo and Hyperion, but still had the habits and the craving left by their old Gods, a fresh breath of reality came with the entrance of Ἥλιος ἀνίκητος Μίθρας, ' Mithras, the Unconquered Sun'. But long before the triumph of Mithraism as the military religion of the Roman frontier, Greek literature is permeated with a kind of intense language about the Sun, which seems derived from Plato.[2] In later times, in the fourth century A. D. for instance, it has absorbed some more full-blooded and less critical element as well.

Secondly, all the seven planets. These had a curious history. The planets were of course divine and living bodies, so much Plato gave us. Then come arguments

---

[1] Mithras was worshipped by the Cilician Pirates conquered by Pompey. Plut., *Vit. Pomp.* 24.

[2] ἔκγονος τοῦ πρώτου θεοῦ. Plato (Diels, 305) ; Stoics, ib. 547, l. 8.

and questions scattered through the Stoic and eclectic
literature. Is it the planet itself that is divine, or is
the planet under the guidance of a divine spirit? The
latter seems to win the day. Anthropomorphism has
stolen back upon us : we can use the old language and
speak simply of the planet Mercury as Ἑρμοῦ ἀστήρ.
It is the star of Hermes, and Hermes is the spirit who
guides it.[1] Even Plato in his old age had much to
say about the souls of the seven planets. Further,
each planet has its sphere. The Earth is in the centre,
then comes the sphere of the Moon, then that of the
Sun, and so on through a range of seven spheres. If
all things are full of gods, as the wise ancients have
said, what about those parts of the sphere in which the
shining planet for the moment is not? Are they without god? Obviously not. The whole sphere is filled
with innumerable spirits everywhere. It is all Hermes,
all Aphrodite. (We are more familiar with the Latin
names, Mercury and Venus.) But one part only is
visible. The voice of one school, as usual, is raised in
opposition. One veteran had seen clearly from the
beginning whither all this sort of thing was sure to lead.
' Epicurus approves none of these things.'[2] It was no
good his having destroyed the old traditional superstition, if people by deifying the stars were to fill the sky

---

[1] Aristotle (Diels, 450). ὅσας δὲ εἶναι τὰς σφαίρας, τοσούτους ὑπάρ-
χειν καὶ τοὺς κινοῦντας θεούς. Chrysippus (Diels, 466) ; Posidonius,
ib. (cf. Plato, Laws, 898 ff.). See Epicurus's Second Letter, especially
Usener, pp. 36–47 = Diog. La. x. 86–104. On the food required
by the heavenly bodies cf. Chrysippus, fr. 658–61, Arnim.

[2] ὁ δὲ Ἐπίκουρος οὐδὲν τούτων ἐγκρίνει. Diels, 307ᵃ 15. Cf.
432ᵃ 10.

with seven times seven as many objects of worship
as had been there before. He allows no *Schwärmerei*
about the stars. They are *not* divine animate beings,
or guided by Gods. Why cannot the astrologers leave
God in peace? When their orbits are irregular it is
not because they are looking for food. They are just
conglomerations of ordinary atoms of air or fire—it
does not matter which. They are not even very
large—only about as large as they look, or perhaps
smaller, since most fires tend to look bigger at a distance. They are not at all certainly everlasting. It is
quite likely that the sun comes to an end every day,
and a new one rises in the morning. All kinds of
explanations are possible, and none certain. Μόνον ὁ
μῦθος ἀπέστω. In any case, as you value your life and
your reason, do not begin making myths about them!

On other lines came what might have been the
effective protest of real Science, when Aristarchus of
Samos (250 B. c.) argued that the earth was not really
the centre of the universe, but revolved round the
Sun. But his hypothesis did not account for the
phenomena as completely as the current theory with
its 'Epicycles'; his fellow astronomers were against
him; Cleanthes the Stoic denounced him for 'disturbing the Hearth of the Universe', and his heresy
made little headway.[1]

The planets in their seven spheres surrounding the
earth continued to be objects of adoration. They had
their special gods or guiding spirits assigned them.
Their ordered movements through space, it was held,

[1] Heath, *Aristarchos of Samos*, pp. 301–10.

produce a vast and eternal harmony. It is beautiful
beyond all earthly music, this Music of the Spheres,
beyond all human dreams of what music might be.
The only pity is that—except for a few individuals in
trances—nobody has ever heard it. Circumstances
seem always to be unfavourable. It may be that we
are too far off, though, considering the vastness of the
orchestra, this seems improbable. More likely we are
merely deaf to it because it never stops and we have
been in the middle of it since we first drew breath.[1]

The planets also become Elements in the Kosmos,
Stoicheia. It is significant that in Hellenistic theology
the word Stoicheion, Element, gets to mean a Daemon
—as Megethos, Greatness, means an Angel.[2] But
behold a mystery ! The word *Stoicheia*, ' elementa ',
had long been used for the Greek A B C, and in
particular for the seven vowels α ε η ι ο υ ω. That is
no chance, no mere coincidence. The vowels are the
mystic signs of the Planets ; they have control over the
planets. Hence strange prayers and magic formulae
innumerable.

Even the way of reckoning time changed under the
influence of the Planets. Instead of the old division of
the month into three periods of nine days, we find
gradually establishing itself the week of seven days with
each day named after its planet, Sun, Moon, Ares,

---

[1] Pythagoras in Diels, p. 555, 20 ; the best criticism is in Aristotle,
De Caelo, chap. 9 (p. 290 b), the fullest account in Macrobius, *Comm.
in Somn. Scipionis*, ii.

[2] See Diels, *Elementum*, 1899, p. 17. These magic letters are still
used in the Roman ritual for the consecration of churches.

Hermes, Zeus, Aphrodite, Kronos. The history of the
Planet week is given by Dio Cassius, xxxvii. 18, in his
account of the Jewish campaign of Pompeius. But
it was not the Jewish week. The Jews scorned such
idolatrous and polytheistic proceedings. It was the
old week of Babylon, the original home of astronomy
and planet-worship.[1]

For here again a great foreign religion came like
water in the desert to minds reluctantly and superficially enlightened, but secretly longing for the old
terrors and raptures from which they had been set free.
Even in the old days Aeschylus had called the planets
' bright potentates, shining in the fire of heaven ', and
Euripides had spoken of the ' shaft hurled from a star '.[2]
But we are told that the first teaching of astrology in
Hellenic lands was in the time of Alexander, when
Bêrôssos the Chaldaean set up a school in Cos and,
according to Seneca, *Belum interpretatus est.* This must
mean that he translated into Greek the ' *Eye of Bel* ',
a treatise in seventy tablets found in the library of
Assur-bani-pal (686–626 B. C.) but composed for Sargon I
in the third millennium B. C. Even the philosopher
Theophrastus is reported by Proclus [3] as saying that
' the most extraordinary thing of his age was the lore
of the Chaldaeans, who foretold not only events of
public interest but even the lives and deaths of

---

[1] A seven-day week was known to Pseudo-Hippocrates περὶ σαρκῶν
ad fin., but the date of that treatise is very uncertain.

[2] Aesch., *Ag.* 6; Eur., *Hip.* 530. Also *Ag.* 365, where ἀστρῶν βέλος
goes together and μήτε πρὸ καιροῦ μήθ᾽ ὕπερ.

[3] Proclus, *In Timaeum*, 285 F; Seneca, *Nat. Quaest.* iii. 29, 1.

individuals '. One wonders slightly whether Theophrastus spoke with as much implicit faith as Proclus suggests. But the chief account is given by Diodorus, ii. 30 (perhaps from Hecataeus).

' Other nations despise the philosophy of Greece. It is so recent and so constantly changing. They have traditions which come from vast antiquity and never change. Notably the Chaldaeans have collected observations of the Stars through long ages, and teach how every event in the heavens has its meaning, as part of the eternal scheme of divine forethought. Especially the seven Wanderers, or Planets, are called by them Hermêneis, Interpreters : and among them the Interpreter in chief is Saturn. Their work is to interpret beforehand τὴν τῶν θεῶν ἔννοιαν, the thought that is in the mind of the Gods. By their risings and settings, and by the colours they assume, the Chaldaeans predict great winds and storms and waves of excessive heat, comets, and earthquakes, and in general all changes fraught with weal or woe not only to nations and regions of the world, but to kings and to ordinary men and women. Beneath the Seven are thirty Gods of Counsel, half below and half above the Earth ; every ten days a Messenger or Angel star passes from above below and another from below above. Above these gods are twelve Masters, who are the twelve signs of the Zodiac ; and the planets pass through all the Houses of these twelve in turn. The Chaldaeans have made prophecies for various kings, such as Alexander who conquered Darius, and Antigonus and Seleucus Nikator, and have always been right. And private persons who have consulted them consider their wisdom as marvellous and above human power.'

Astrology fell upon the Hellenistic mind as a new disease falls upon some remote island people. The

tomb of Ozymandias, as described by Diodorus
(i. 49, 5) was covered with astrological symbols, and
that of Antiochus I, which has been discovered in
Commagene, is of the same character. It was natural
for monarchs to believe that the stars watched over
them. But every one was ready to receive the germ.
The Epicureans, of course, held out, and so did
Panaetius, the coolest head among the Stoics. But
the Stoics as a whole gave way. They formed with
good reason the leading school of philosophy, and it
would have been a service to mankind if they had
resisted. But they were already committed to a belief
in the deity of the stars and to the doctrine of Heimarmenê, or Destiny. They believed in the pervading
Pronoia,[1] or Forethought, of the divine mind, and in
the Συμπάθεια τῶν ὅλων—the Sympathy of all Creation,[2] whereby whatever happens to any one part,
however remote or insignificant, affects all the rest.
It seemed only a natural and beautiful illustration of
this Sympathy that the movements of the Stars should
be bound up with the sufferings of man. They also
appealed to the general belief in prophecy and divination.[3] If a prophet can foretell that such and such an
event will happen, then it is obviously fated to happen.

[1] Chrysippus, 1187–95. Esse divinationem si di sint et providentia.

[2] Cicero, De Nat. De. iii. 11, 28; especially De Divinatione, ii. 14, 34;
60, 124; 69, 142. 'Qua ex coniunctione naturae et quasi concentu
atque consensu, quam συμπάθειαν Graeci appellant, convenire potest
aut fissum iecoris cum lucello meo aut meus quaesticulus cum caelo,
terra rerumque natura?' asks the sceptic in the second of these
passages.

[3] Chrysippus, 939–44. Vaticinatio probat fati necessitatem.

Foreknowledge implies Predestination. This belief in prophecy was, in reality, a sort of appeal to fact and to common sense. People could produce then, as they can now, a large number of striking cases of second sight, presentiment, clairvoyance, actual prophecy and the like ; [1] and it was more difficult then to test them.

The argument involved Stoicism with some questionable allies. Epicureans and sceptics of the Academy might well mock at the sight of a great man like Chrysippus or Posidonius resting an important part of his religion on the undetected frauds of a shady Levantine ' medium '. Still the Stoics could not but welcome the arrival of a system of prophecy and predestination which, however the incredulous might rail at it, possessed at least great antiquity and great stores of learning, which was respectable, recondite, and in a way sublime.

In all the religious systems of later antiquity, if I mistake not, the Seven Planets play some lordly or terrifying part. The great Mithras Liturgy, unearthed by Dieterich from a magical papyrus in Paris,[2] repeatedly confronts the worshipper with the seven vowels as names of ' the Seven Deathless Kosmokratores ', or Lords of the Universe, and seems, under their influence, to go off into its ' Seven Maidens with heads of serpents, in white raiment ', and its divers other Sevens.

[1] Chrysippus, 1214, 1200-6.

[2] *Eine Mithrasliturgie*, 1903. The MS. is 574 Supplément grec de la Bibl. Nationale. The formulae of various religions were used as instruments of magic, as our own witches used the Lord's Prayer backwards.

The various Hermetic and Mithraic communities, the
Naassenes described by Hippolytus,[1] and other Gnostic
bodies, authors like Macrobius and even Cicero in his
Somnium Scipionis, are full of the influence of the seven
planets and of the longing to escape beyond them. For
by some simple psychological law the stars which have
inexorably pronounced our fate, and decreed, or at
least registered the decree, that in spite of all striving
we must needs tread their prescribed path ; still more
perhaps, the Stars who know in the midst of our
laughter how that laughter will end, become inevitably
powers of evil rather than good, beings malignant as
well as pitiless, making life a vain thing. And Saturn,
the chief of them, becomes the most malignant. To
some of the Gnostics he becomes Jaldabaoth, the Lion-
headed God, the evil Jehovah.[2] The religion of later
antiquity is overpoweringly absorbed in plans of escape
from the prison of the seven planets.

In author after author, in one community after
another, the subject recurs. And on the whole there
is the same answer. Here on the earth we are the
sport of Fate ; nay, on the earth itself we are worse
off still. We are beneath the Moon, and beneath the
Moon there is not only Fate but something more
unworthy and equally malignant, Chance—to say
nothing of damp and the ills of earth and bad daemons.
Above the Moon there is no chance, only Necessity ;

---

[1] *Refutatio Omnium Haeresium*, v. 7. They worshipped the Serpent,
Nāhāsh (נָחָשׁ).

[2] Bousset, p. 351. The hostility of Zoroastrianism to the old
Babylonian planet gods was doubtless at work also. Ib. pp. 37-46.

there is the will of the other six Kosmokratores, Rulers
of the Universe. But above them all there is an Eighth
region—they call it simply the Ogdoas—the home of
the ultimate God,[1] whatever He is named, whose being
was before the Kosmos. In this Sphere is true Being
and Freedom. And more than freedom, there is the
ultimate Union with God. For that spark of divine
life which is man's soul is not merely, as some have
said, an ἀπόρροια τῶν ἄστρων, an effluence of the stars :
it comes direct from the first and ultimate God, the
Alpha and Omega, who is beyond the Planets. Though
the Kosmokratores cast us to and fro like their slaves
or dead chattels, in soul at least we are of equal birth
with them. The Mithraic votary, when their wrathful
and tremendous faces break in upon his vision, answers
them unterrified : ἐγώ εἰμι σύμπλανος ὑμῖν ἀστήρ,
' I am your fellow wanderer, your fellow Star.' The
Orphic carried to the grave on his golden scroll the
same boast : first, ' I am the child of Earth and of the
starry Heaven ' ; then later, ' I too am become God '.[2]
The Gnostic writings consist largely of charms to be
uttered by the Soul to each of the Planets in turn,
as it pursues its perilous path past all of them to its
ultimate home.

That journey awaits us after death ; but in the
meantime? In the meantime there are initiations,
sacraments, mystic ways of communion with God.
To see God face to face is, to the ordinary unprepared
man, sheer death. But to see Him after due purifica-

---

[1] Or, in some Gnostic systems, of the Mother.

[2] Harrison, *Prolegomena*, Appendix on the Orphic tablets.

tion, to be led to Him along the true Way by an initiating Priest, is the ultimate blessing of human life. It is to die and be born again. There were regular official initiations. We have one in the Mithras-Liturgy, more than one in the Corpus Hermeticum. Apuleius [1] tells us at some length, though in guarded language, how he was initiated to Isis and became ' her image '. After much fasting, clad in holy garments and led by the High Priest, he crossed the threshold of Death and passed through all the Elements. The Sun shone upon him at midnight, and he saw the Gods of Heaven and of Hades. In the morning he was clad in the Robe of Heaven, set up on a pedestal in front of the Goddess and worshipped by the congregation as a God. He had been made one with Osiris or Horus or whatever name it pleased that Sun-God to be called. Apuleius does not reveal it.

There were also, of course, the irregular personal initiations and visions of god vouchsafed to persons of special prophetic powers. St. Paul, we may remember, knew personally a man who had actually been snatched up into the Third Heaven, and another who was similarly rapt into Paradise, where he heard unspeakable words ; [2] whether in the body or not, the apostle leaves undecided. He himself on the road to Damascus had seen the Christ in glory, not after the

[1] Ap. *Metamorphoses*, xi.

[2] 2 Cor. xii. 2 and 3 (he may be referring in veiled language to himself) ; Gal. i. 12 ff. ; Acts ix. 1–22. On the difference of tone and fidelity between the Epistles and the Acts see the interesting remarks of Prof. P. Gardner, *The Religious Experience of St. Paul*, pp. 5 ff.

flesh. The philosopher Plotinus, so his disciple tells us, was united with God in trance four times in five years.[1]

We seem to have travelled far from the simplicity of early Greek religion. Yet, apart always from Plotinus, who is singularly aloof, most of the movement has been a reaction under Oriental and barbarous influences towards the most primitive pre-Hellenic cults. The union of man with God came regularly through *Ekstasis*—the soul must get clear of its body—and *Enthousiasmos*—the God must enter and dwell inside the worshipper. But the means to this union, while sometimes allegorized and spiritualized to the last degree, are sometimes of the most primitive sort. The vagaries of religious emotion are apt to reach very low as well as very high in the scale of human nature. Certainly the primitive Thracian savages, who drank themselves mad with the hot blood of their God-beast,

[1] Porphyry, *Vita Plotini*, 23. ' We have explained that he was good and gentle, mild and merciful; we who lived with him could feel it. We have said that he was vigilant and pure of soul, and always striving towards the Divine, which with all his soul he loved. . . . And thus it happened to this extraordinary man, constantly lifting himself up towards the first and transcendent God by thought and the ways explained by Plato in the *Symposium*, that there actually came a vision of that God who is without shape or form, established above the understanding and all the intelligible world. To whom I, Porphyry, being now in my sixty-eighth year, profess that I once drew near and was made one with him. At any rate he appeared to Plotinus " a goal close at hand ". For his whole end and goal was to be made One and draw near to the supreme God. And he attained that goal four times, I think, while I was living with him—not potentially but in actuality, though an actuality which surpasses speech.'

would have been quite at home in some of these rituals, though in others they would have been put off with some substitute for the actual blood. The primitive priestesses who waited in a bridal chamber for the Divine Bridegroom, even the Cretan Kourêtes with their Zeus Kourês [1] and those strange hierophants of the ' Men's House ' whose initiations are written on the rocks of Thera, would have found rites very like their own reblossoming on earth after the fall of Hellenism. ' Prepare thyself as a bride to receive her bridegroom,' says Markos the Gnostic,[2] ' that thou mayst be what I am and I what thou art.' ' I in thee, and thou in me ! ' is the ecstatic cry of one of the Hermes liturgies. Before that the prayer has been ' Enter into me as a babe into the womb of a woman '.[3]

In almost all the liturgies that I have read need is felt for a mediator between the seeker after God and his goal. Mithras himself was a Mesîtês, a Mediator, between Ormuzd and Ahriman, but the ordinary mediator is more like an interpreter or an adept with inner knowledge which he reveals to the outsider. The circumstances out of which these systems grew have left their mark on the new gods themselves. As usual, the social structure of the worshippers is reflected in their objects of worship. When the Chaldaeans came to Cos, when the Thracians in the Piraeus set up their

---

[1] *C. I. G.*, vol. xii, fasc. 3 ; and Bethe in *Rhein. Mus.*, N. F., xlii, 438-75.   [2] Irenaeus, i. 13, 3.

[3] Bousset, chap. vii ; Reitzenstein, *Mysterienreligionen*, pp. 20 ff., with excursus ; *Poimandres*, 226 ff. ; Dieterich, *Mithrasliturgie*, pp. 121 ff.

national worship of Bendis, when the Egyptians in the same port founded their society for the Egyptian ritual of Isis, when the Jews at Assuan in the fifth century B.C. established their own temple, in each case there would come proselytes to whom the truth must be explained and interpreted, sometimes perhaps softened. And in each case there is behind the particular priest or initiator there present some greater authority in the land he comes from. Behind any explanation that can be made in the Piraeus, there is a deeper and higher explanation known only to the great master in Jerusalem, in Egypt, in Babylon, or perhaps in some unexplored and ever-receding region of the east. This series of revelations, one behind the other, is a characteristic of all these mixed Graeco-Oriental religions.

Most of the Hermetic treatises are put in the form of initiations or lessons revealed by a ' father ' to a ' son ', by Ptah to Hermes, by Hermes to Thoth or Asclepios, and by one of them to us. It was an ancient formula, a natural vehicle for traditional wisdom in Egypt, where the young priest became regularly the ' son ' of the old priest. It is a form that we find in Greece itself as early as Euripides, whose Melanippe says of her cosmological doctrines,

' It is not my word but my Mother's word.' [1]

It was doubtless the language of the old Medicine-Man to his disciple. In one fine liturgy Thoth wrestles with Hermes in agony of spirit, till Hermes is forced to reveal to him the path to union with God which

---

[1] Eur. fr. 484.

he himself has trodden before. At the end of the
Mithras liturgy the devotee who has passed through
the mystic ordeals and seen his god face to face, is told :
' After this you can show the way to others.'

But this leads us to the second great division of our
subject. We turn from the phenomena of the sky to
those of the soul.

If what I have written elsewhere is right, one of the
greatest works of the Hellenic spirit, and especially of
fifth-century Athens, was to insist on what seems to
us such a commonplace truism, the difference between
Man and God. Sophrosynê in religion was the message of the classical age. But the ages before and after
had no belief in such a lesson. The old Medicine-Man
was perhaps himself the first *Theos*. At any rate the
primeval kings and queens were treated as divine.[1] Just
for a few great generations, it would seem, humanity
rose to a sufficient height of self-criticism and self-
restraint to reject these dreams of self-abasement or
megalomania. But the effort was too great for the
average world ; and in a later age nearly all the kings
and rulers—all people in fact who can command an
adequate number of flatterers—become divine beings
again. Let us consider how it came about.

First there was the explicit recognition by the
soberest philosophers of the divine element in man's

---

[1] *R. G. E.*[3], pp. 135–40. I do not touch on the political side of this
apotheosis of Hellenistic kings ; it is well brought out in Ferguson's
Hellenistic Athens, e. g. p. 108 f., also p. 11 f. and note. Antigonus
Gonatas refused to be worshipped (Tarn, p. 250 f.). For Sallustius's
opinion, see below, p. 266, chap. xviii *ad fin.*

soul.[1] Aristotle himself built an altar to Plato. He did nothing superstitious ; he did not call Plato a god, but we can see from his beautiful elegy to Eudemus, that he naturally and easily used language of worship which would seem a little strange to us. It is the same emotion—a noble and just emotion on the whole—which led the philosophic schools to treat their founders as ' heroes ', and which has peopled most of Europe and Asia with the memories and the worship of saints. But we should remember that only a rare mind will make its divine man of such material as Plato. The common way to dazzle men's eyes is a more brutal and obvious one.

To people who were at all accustomed to the conception of a God-Man it was difficult not to feel that the conception was realized in Alexander. His tremendous power, his brilliant personality, his achievements beggaring the fables of the poets, put people in the right mind for worship. Then came the fact that the kings whom he conquered were, as a matter of fact, mostly regarded by their subjects as divine beings.[2] It was easy, it was almost inevitable, for those who worshipped the ' God '[3] Darius to feel that it was no man but a greater god who had overthrown

[1] Cf. ψυχὴ οἰκητήριον δαίμονος, Democr. 171, Diels, and Alcmaeon is said by Cicero to have attributed divinity to the Stars and the Soul. Melissus and Zeno θείας οἴεται τὰς ψυχάς. The phrase τινὲς τὴν ψυχὴν δύναμιν ἀπὸ τῶν ἄστρων ῥέουσαν, Diels 651, must refer to some Gnostic sect.

[2] See for instance Frazer, *Golden Bough*[3], part I, i. 417–19.

[3] Aesch. *Pers.* 157, 644 (θεός), 642 (δαίμων). Mr. Bevan however suspects that Aeschylus misunderstood his Persian sources : see his article on ' Deification ' in Hastings's *Dictionary of Religion*.

Darius. The incense which had been burned before those conquered gods was naturally offered to their conqueror. He did not refuse it. It was not good policy to do so, and self-depreciation is not apt to be one of the weaknesses of the born ruler.[1] But besides all this, if you are to judge a God by his fruits, what God could produce better credentials? Men had often seen Zeus defied with impunity; they had seen faithful servants of Apollo come to bad ends. But those who defied Alexander, however great they might be, always rued their defiance, and those who were faithful to him always received their reward. With his successors the worship became more official. Seleucus, Ptolemaeus, Antigonus, Demetrius, all in different degrees and different styles are deified by the acclamations of adoring subjects. Ptolemy Philadelphus seems to have been the first to claim definite divine honours during his own life. On the death of his wife in 271 he proclaimed her deity and his own as well in the worship of the Theoi Adelphoi, the ' Gods Brethren '. Of course there was flattery in all this, ordinary self-interested lying flattery, and its inevitable accompaniment, megalomania. Any reading of the personal history of the Ptolemies, the Seleucidae or the Caesars shows it. But that is not the whole explanation.

---

[1] Cf. Aristotle on the Μεγαλόψυχος, *Eth. Nic.* 1123 b. 15. εἰ δὲ δὴ μεγάλων ἑαυτὸν ἀξιοῖ ἄξιος ὤν, καὶ μάλιστα τῶν μεγίστων, περὶ ἓν μάλιστα ἂν εἴη. . . . μέγιστον δὲ τοῦτ' ἂν θείημεν ὃ τοῖς θεοῖς ἀπονέμομεν. But these kings clearly transgressed the mean. For the satirical comments of various public men in Athens see Ed. Meyer, *Kleine Schriften*, 301 ff., 330.

One of the characteristics of the period of the Diadochi is the accumulation of capital and military force in the hands of individuals. The Ptolemies and Seleucidae had at any moment at their disposal powers very much greater than any Pericles or Nicias or Lysander.[1] The folk of the small cities of the Aegean hinterlands must have felt towards these great strangers almost as poor Indian peasants in time of flood and famine feel towards an English official. There were men now on earth who could do the things that had hitherto been beyond the power of man. Were several cities thrown down by earthquake; here was one who by his nod could build them again. Famines had always occurred and been mostly incurable. Here was one who could without effort allay a famine. Provinces were harried and wasted by habitual wars : the eventual conqueror had destroyed whole provinces in making the wars ; now, as he had destroyed, he could also save. ' What do you mean by a god,' the simple man might say, ' if these men are not gods ? The only difference is that these gods are visible, and the old gods no man has seen.'

The titles assumed by all the divine kings tell the story clearly. Antiochus Epiphanês—' the god made manifest ' ; Ptolemaios Euergetês, Ptolemaios Sôtêr. Occasionally we have a Keraunos or a Nikator, a ' Thunderbolt ' or a ' God of Mana ', but mostly it is Sôtêr, Euergetês and Epiphanês, the Saviour, the Benefactor, the God made manifest, in constant alternation. In the honorific inscriptions and in the

[1] Lysander too had altars raised to him by some Asiatic cities.

writings of the learned, philanthropy (φιλανθρωπία) is by far the most prominent characteristic of the God upon earth. Was it that people really felt that to save or benefit mankind was a more godlike thing than to blast and destroy them? Philosophers have generally said that, and the vulgar pretended to believe them. It was at least politic, when ministering to the half-insane pride of one of these princes, to remind him of his mercy rather than of his wrath.

Wendland in his brilliant book, *Hellenistisch-römische Kultur*, calls attention to an inscription of the year 196 B. C. in honour of the young Ptolemaios Epiphanês, who was made manifest at the age of twelve years.[1] It is a typical document of Graeco-Egyptian king-worship:

' In the reign of the young king by inheritance from his Father, Lord of the Diadems, great in glory, pacificator of Egypt and pious towards the gods, superior over his adversaries, Restorer of the life of man, Lord of the Periods of Thirty Years, like Hephaistos the Great, King like the Sun, the Great King of the Upper and Lower Lands; offspring of the Gods of the Love of the Father, whom Hephaistos has approved, to whom the Sun has given Victory; living image of Zeus; Son of the Sun, Ptolemaios the ever-living, beloved by Phtha; in the ninth year of Aëtos son of Aëtos, Priest of Alexander and the Gods Saviours and the Gods Brethren and the Gods Benefactors and the Gods of the Love of the Father and the God Manifest for whom thanks be given: '

[1] Dittenberger, *Inscr. Orientis Graeci*, 90; Wendland, *Hellenistisch-römische Kultur*, 1907, p. 74 f. and notes.

The Priests who came to his coronation ceremony at Memphis proclaim :

' Seeing that King Ptolemaios ever-living, beloved of Phtha, God Manifest for whom Thanks be given, born of King Ptolemaios and Queen Arsinoe, the Gods of the Love of the Father, has done many benefactions to the Temples and those in them and all those beneath his rule, being from the beginning God born of God and Goddess, like Horus son of Isis and Osiris, who came to the help of his father Osiris (and ?) in his benevolent disposition towards the Gods has consecrated to the temples revenues of silver and of corn, and has undergone many expenses in order to lead Egypt into the sunlight and give peace to the Temples, and has with all his powers shown love of mankind.'

When the people of Lycopolis revolted, we hear :

' in a short time he took the city by storm and slew all the Impious who dwelt in it, even as Hermes and Horus, son of Isis and Osiris, conquered those who of old revolted in the same regions . . . in return for which the Gods have granted him Health Victory Power and all other good things, the Kingdom remaining to him and his sons for time everlasting.' [1]

---

[1] Several of the phrases are interesting. The last gift of the heavenly gods to this Theos is the old gift of Mana. In Hesiod it was Κάρτος τε Βίη τε, the two ministers who are never away from the King Zeus. In Aeschylus it was Kratos and Bia who subdue Prometheus. In Tyrtaeus it was Νίκη καὶ Κάρτος. In other inscriptions of the Ptolemaic age it is Σωτηρία καὶ Νίκη or Σωτηρία καὶ Νίκη αἰώνιος. In the current Christian liturgies it is ' the Kingdom, the Power, and the Glory '. R. G. E.³, p. 135, n. The new conception, as always, is rooted in the old. 'The Gods Saviours, Brethren ', &c., are of course Ptolemy Soter, Ptolemy Philadelphus, &c., and their Queens. The phrases εἰκὼν ζῶσα τοῦ Διός, υἱὸς τοῦ Ἡλίου, ἠγαπημένος ὑπὸ τοῦ Φθᾶ, are

The conclusion which the Priests draw from these facts is that the young king's titles and honours are insufficient and should be increased. It is a typical and terribly un-Hellenic document of the Hellenistic God-man in his appearance as King.

Now the early successors of Alexander mostly professed themselves members of the Stoic school, and in the mouth of a Stoic this doctrine of the potential divinity of man was an inspiring one. To them virtue was the really divine thing in man; and the most divine kind of virtue was that of helping humanity. To love and help humanity is, according to Stoic doctrine, the work and the very essence of God. If you take away Pronoia from God, says Chrysippus,[1] it is like taking away light and heat from fire. This doctrine is magnificently expressed by Pliny in a phrase that is probably translated from Posidonius: 'God is the helping of man by man; and that is the way to eternal glory.'[2]

The conception took root in the minds of many Romans. A great Roman governor often had the chance of thus helping humanity on a vast scale, and liked to think that such a life opened the way to heaven. 'One should conceive', says Cicero (*Tusc.* i. 32), 'the gods as like men who feel themselves born for the work

characteristic of the religious language of this period. Cf. also Col. i. 14, εἰκὼν τοῦ θεοῦ τοῦ ἀοράτου; 2 Cor. iv. 4; Ephes. i. 5, 6.

[1] Fr. 1118, Arnim. Cf. Antipater, fr. 33, 34, τὸ εὐποιητικόν is part of the definition of Deity.

[2] Plin., *Nat. Hist.* ii. 7, 18. Deus est mortali iuvare mortalem et haec ad aeternam gloriam via. Cf. also the striking passages from Cicero and others in Wendland, p. 85, n. 2.

of helping, defending, and saving humanity. Hercules has passed into the number of the gods. He would never have so passed if he had not built up that road for himself while he was among mankind.'

I have been using some rather late authors, though the ideas seem largely to come from Posidonius.[1] But before Posidonius the sort of fact on which we have been dwelling had had its influence on religious speculation. When Alexander made his conquering journey to India and afterwards was created a god, it was impossible not to reflect that almost exactly the same story was related in myth about Dionysus. Dionysus had started from India and travelled in the other direction : that was the only difference. A flood of light seemed to be thrown on all the traditional mythology, which, of course, had always been a puzzle to thoughtful men. It was impossible to believe it as it stood, and yet hard—in an age which had not the conception of any science of mythology—to think it was all a mass of falsehood, and the great Homer and Hesiod no better than liars. But the generation which witnessed the official deification of the various Seleucidae and Ptolemies seemed suddenly to see light. The traditional gods, from Heracles and Dionysus up to Zeus and Cronos and even Ouranos, were simply old-world rulers and benefactors of mankind, who had, by their own insistence or the gratitude of their subjects,

---

[1] The Stoic philosopher, teaching at Rhodes, *c.* 100 B. C. A man of immense knowledge and strong religious emotions, he moved the Stoa in the direction of Oriental mysticism. See Schwartz's sketch in *Characterköpfe*[2], pp. 89–98. Also Norden's *Commentary on Aeneid* vi.

been transferred to the ranks of heaven. For that is the exact meaning of making them divine : they are classed among the true immortals, the Sun and Moon and Stars and Corn and Wine, and the everlasting elements.

The philosophic romance of Euhemerus, published early in the third century B. C., had instantaneous success and enormous influence.[1] It was one of the first Greek books translated into Latin, and became long afterwards a favourite weapon of the Christian fathers in their polemics against polytheism. ' Euhemerism ' was, on the face of it, a very brilliant theory ; and it had, as we have noticed, a special appeal for the Romans.

Yet, if such a conception might please the leisure of a statesman, it could hardly satisfy the serious thought of a philosopher or a religious man. If man's soul really holds a fragment of God and is itself a divine being, its godhead cannot depend on the possession of great riches and armies and organized subordinates. If ' the helping of man by man is God ', the help in question cannot be material help. The religion which ends in deifying only kings and millionaires may be vulgarly popular but is self-condemned.

As a matter of fact the whole tendency of Greek philosophy after Plato, with some illustrious exceptions, especially among the Romanizing Stoics, was away from the outer world towards the world of the soul. We find in the religious writings of this period that the

---

[1] Jacoby in Pauly-Wissowa's *Realencyclopädie*, vi. 954. It was called Ἱερὰ Ἀναγραφή.

real Saviour of men is not he who protects them against earthquake and famine, but he who in some sense saves their souls. He reveals to them the *Gnôsis Theou*, the Knowledge of God. The 'knowledge' in question is not a mere intellectual knowledge. It is a complete union, a merging of beings. And, as we have always to keep reminding our cold modern intelligence, he who has 'known' God is himself thereby deified. He is the Image of God, the Son of God, in a sense he *is* God.[1] The stratum of ideas described in the first of the studies will explain the ease with which transition took place. The worshipper of Bacchos became Bacchos simply enough, because in reality the God Bacchos was originally only the projection of the human Bacchoi. And in the Hellenistic age the notion of these secondary mediating gods was made easier by the analogy of the human interpreters. Of course, we have abundant instances of actual preachers and miracle-workers who on their own authority posed, and were accepted, as gods. The adventure of Paul and Barnabas at Lystra[2] shows how easily such things could happen. But as a rule, I suspect, the most zealous priest or preacher preferred to have his God in the background. He preaches, he heals the sick and casts out devils, not in his own name but in the name of One who sent him. This actual present

---

[1] Cf. Plotin. *Enn.* I. ii. 6 ἀλλ' ἡ σπουδὴ οὐκ ἔξω ἁμαρτίας εἶναι, ἀλλὰ θεὸν εἶναι.

[2] Acts xiv. 12. They called Barnabas Zeus and Paul Hermes, because he was ὁ ἡγούμενος τοῦ λόγου.—Paul also writes to the Galatians (iv. 14): 'Ye received me *as a messenger of God, as Jesus Christ.*'

priest who initiates you or me is himself already an
Image of God ; but above him there are greater and
wiser priests, above them others, and above all there is
the one eternal Divine Mediator, who being in perfection both man and God can alone fully reveal God to
man, and lead man's soul up the heavenly path, beyond
Change and Fate and the Houses of the Seven Rulers,
to its ultimate peace. I have seen somewhere a
Gnostic or early Christian emblem which indicates
this doctrine. Some Shepherd or Saviour stands, his
feet on the earth, his head towering above the planets,
lifting his follower in his outstretched arms.

The Gnostics are still commonly thought of as a body
of Christian heretics. In reality there were Gnostic
sects scattered over the Hellenistic world before
Christianity as well as after. They must have been
established in Antioch and probably in Tarsus well
before the days of Paul or Apollos. Their Saviour,
like the Jewish Messiah, was established in men's minds
before the Saviour of the Christians. ' If we look
close ', says Professor Bousset, ' the result emerges with
great clearness, that the figure of the Redeemer as such
did not wait for Christianity to force its way into the
religion of Gnôsis, but was already present there under
various forms.' [1] He occurs notably in two pre-
Christian documents, discovered by the keen analysis
and profound learning of Dr. Reitzenstein : the
Poimandres revelation printed in the *Corpus Hermeticum*, and the sermon of the Naassenes in Hippolytus,
Refutatio Omnium Haeresium, which is combined with

[1] Bousset, p. 238.

Attis-worship.[1] The violent anti-Jewish bias of most
of the sects—they speak of 'the accursed God of the
Jews' and identify him with Saturn and the Devil—
points on the whole to pre-Christian conditions; and
a completely non-Christian standpoint is still visible
in the Mandaean and Manichean systems.

Their Redeemer is descended by a fairly clear
genealogy from the 'Tritos Sôtêr' of early Greece,
contaminated with similar figures, like Attis and
Adonis from Asia Minor, Osiris from Egypt, and
the special Jewish conception of the Messiah of the
Chosen people. He has various names, which the name
of Jesus or 'Christos', 'the Anointed', tends gradually
to supersede. Above all he is, in some sense, Man, or
'the Second Man' or 'the Son of Man'. The origin
of this phrase needs a word of explanation. Since the
ultimate unseen God, spirit though He is, made Man
in His image, since holy men (and divine kings) are
images of God, it follows that He is Himself Man. He
is the real, the ultimate, the perfect and eternal Man,
of whom all bodily men are feeble copies. He is also
the Father; the Saviour is his Son, 'the Image of the
Father', 'the Second Man', 'the Son of Man'. The
method in which he performs his mystery of Redemp-
tion varies. It is haunted by the memory of the old
Suffering and Dying God, of whom we spoke in the
first of these studies. It is vividly affected by the ideal
'Righteous Man' of Plato, who 'shall be scourged,
tortured, bound, his eyes burnt out, and at last, after

[1] Hippolytus, 134, 90 ff., text in Reitzenstein's *Poimandres*, pp.
83–98.

suffering every evil, shall be impaled or crucified '.[1]
But in the main he descends, of his free will or by the
eternal purpose of the Father, from Heaven through
the spheres of all the Archontes or Kosmokratores,
the planets, to save mankind, or sometimes to save the
fallen Virgin, the Soul, Wisdom, or ' the Pearl '.[2] The
Archontes let him pass because he is disguised ; they
do not know him (cf. 1 Cor. ii. 7 ff.). When his work
is done he ascends to Heaven to sit by the side of the
Father in glory ; he conquers the Archontes, leads them
captive in his triumph, strips them of their armour
(Col. ii. 15 ; cf. the previous verse), sometimes even
crucifies them for ever in their places in the sky.[3] The
epistles to the Colossians and the Ephesians are much
influenced by these doctrines. Paul himself constantly
uses the language of them, but in the main we find
him discouraging the excesses of superstition, reform-
ing, ignoring, rejecting. His Jewish blood was perhaps
enough to keep him to strict monotheism. Though he
admits Angels and Archontes, Principalities and Powers,
he scorns the Elements and he seems deliberately to
reverse the doctrine of the first and second Man.[4] He
says nothing about the Trinity of Divine Beings that
was usual in Gnosticism, nothing about the Divine

---

[1] *Republic*, 362 A. Ἀνασχινδυλεύω is said to = ἀνασκολοπίζω, which
is used both for ' impale ' and ' crucify '. The two were alternative
forms of the most slavish and cruel capital punishment, impalement
being mainly Persian, crucifixion Roman.

[2] See *The Hymn of the Soul*, attributed to the Gnostic Bardesanes,
edited by A. A. Bevan, Cambridge, 1897.

[3] Bousset cites Acta Archelai 8, and Epiphanius, *Haeres.* 66, 32.

[4] Gal. iv. 9 ; 1 Cor. xv. 21 f., 47 ; Rom. v. 12–18.

Mother. His mind, for all its vehement mysticism, has something of that clean antiseptic quality that makes such early Christian works as the Octavius of Minucius Felix and the Epistle to Diognetus so infinitely refreshing. He is certainly one of the great figures in Greek literature, but his system lies outside the subject of this essay. We are concerned only with those last manifestations of Hellenistic religion which probably formed the background of his philosophy. It is a strange experience, and it shows what queer stuff we humans are made of, to study these obscure congregations, drawn from the proletariate of the Levant, superstitious, charlatan-ridden, and helplessly ignorant, who still believed in Gods begetting children of mortal mothers, who took the ' Word ', the ' Spirit ', and the ' Divine Wisdom ', to be persons called by those names, and turned the Immortality of the Soul into ' the standing up of the corpses ' ; [1] and to reflect that it was these who held the main road of advance towards the greatest religion of the western world.

I have tried to sketch in outline the main forms of belief to which Hellenistic philosophy moved or drifted. Let me dwell for a few pages more upon the characteristic method by which it reached them. It may be summed up in one word, Allegory. All Hellenistic philosophy from the first Stoics onward is permeated by allegory. It is applied to Homer, to the religious traditions, to the ancient rituals, to the whole world. To Sallustius after the end of our period

---

[1] ἡ ἀνάστασις τῶν νεκρῶν. Cf. Acts xvii. 32.

the whole material world is only a great myth, a thing whose value lies not in itself but in the spiritual meaning which it hides and reveals. To Cleanthes at the beginning of it the Universe was a mystic pageant, in which the immortal stars were the dancers and the Sun the priestly torch-bearer.[1] Chrysippus reduced the Homeric gods to physical or ethical principles ; and Crates, the great critic, applied allegory in detail to his interpretation of the all-wise poet.[2] We possess two small but complete treatises which illustrate well the results of this tendency, Cornutus περὶ θεῶν and the *Homeric Allegories* of Heraclitus, a brilliant little work of the first century B. C. I will not dwell upon details : they are abundantly accessible and individually often ridiculous. A by-product of the same activity is the mystic treatment of language : a certain Titan in Hesiod is named Koios. Why ? Because the Titans are the elements and one of them is naturally the element of Κοιότης, the Ionic Greek for ' Quality '. The Egyptian Isis is derived from the root of the Greek εἰδέναι, Knowledge, and the Egyptian Osiris from the Greek ὅσιος and ἱρός (' holy ' and ' sacred ', or perhaps more exactly ' lawful ' and ' *tabu* '). Is this totally absurd ? I think not. If all human language is, as most of these thinkers believed, a divine institution, a cup filled to the brim with divine meaning, so that by reflecting deeply upon a word

---

[1] Cleanthes, 538, Arnim ; Diels, p. 592, 30. Cf. Philolaus, Diels, p. 336 f.

[2] See especially the interpretation of Nestor's Cup, Athenaeus, pp. 489 c. ff.

a pious philosopher can reach the secret that it holds, then there is no difficulty whatever in supposing that the special secret held by an Egyptian word may be found in Greek, or the secret of a Greek word in Babylonian. Language is One. The Gods who made all these languages equally could use them all, and wind them all intricately in and out, for the building up of their divine enigma.

We must make a certain effort of imagination to understand this method of allegory. It is not the frigid thing that it seems to us. In the first place, we should remember that, as applied to the ancient literature and religious ritual, allegory was at least a *vera causa*—it was a phenomenon which actually existed. Heraclitus of Ephesus is an obvious instance. He deliberately expressed himself in language which should not be understood of the vulgar, and which bore a hidden meaning to his disciples. Pythagoras did the same. The prophets and religious writers must have done so to an even greater extent.[1] And we know enough of the history of ritual to be sure that a great deal of it is definitely allegorical. The Hellenistic Age did not wantonly invent the theory of allegory.

And secondly, we must remember what states of mind tend especially to produce this kind of belief. They are not contemptible states of mind. It needs only a strong idealism with which the facts of experience clash, and allegory follows almost of necessity.

[1] I may refer to the learned and interesting remarks on the Esoteric Style in Prof. Margoliouth's edition of Aristotle's *Poetics*. It is not, of course, the same as Allegory.

The facts cannot be accepted as they are. They must needs be explained as meaning something different.

Take an earnest Stoic or Platonist, a man of fervid mind, who is possessed by the ideals of his philosophy and at the same time feels his heart thrilled by the beauty of the old poetry. What is he to do? On one side he can find Zoilus, or Plato himself, or the Cynic preachers, condemning Homer and the poets without remorse, as teachers of foolishness. He can treat poetry as the English Puritans treated the stage. But is that a satisfactory solution? Remember that these generations were trained habitually to give great weight to the voice of their inner consciousness, and the inner consciousness of a sensitive man cries out that any such solution is false : that Homer is not a liar, but noble and great, as our fathers have always taught us. On the other side comes Heraclitus the allegorist. 'If Homer used no allegories he committed all impieties.' On this theory the words can be allowed to possess all their old beauty and magic, but an inner meaning is added quite different from that which they bear on the surface. It may, very likely, be a duller and less poetic meaning ; but I am not sure that the verses will not gain by the mere process of brooding study fully as much as they lose by the ultimate badness of the interpretation. Anyhow, that was the road followed. The men of whom I speak were not likely to give up any experience that seemed to make the world more godlike or to feed their spiritual and emotional cravings. They left that to the barefooted cynics. They craved poetry and they craved philosophy ; if the two spoke

like enemies, their words must needs be explained away
by one who loved both.

The same process was applied to the world itself.
Something like it is habitually applied by the religious
idealists of all ages. A fundamental doctrine of
Stoicism and most of the idealist creeds was the
perfection and utter blessedness of the world, and
the absolute fulfilment of the purpose of God. Now
obviously this belief was not based on experience. The
poor world, to do it justice amid all its misdoings, has
never lent itself to any such barefaced deception as
that. No doubt it shrieked against the doctrine then,
as loud as it has always shrieked, so that even a Posidonian or a Pythagorean, his ears straining for the
music of the spheres, was sometimes forced to listen.
And what was his answer? It is repeated in all the
literature of these sects. ' Our human experience is
so small : the things of the earth may be bad and more
than bad, but, ah ! if you only went beyond the
Moon ! That is where the true Kosmos begins.' And,
of course, if we did ever go there, we all know they
would say it began beyond the Sun. Idealism of a certain type will have its way ; if hard life produces an
ounce or a pound or a million tons of fact in the scale
against it, it merely dreams of infinite millions in its
own scale, and the enemy is outweighed and smothered.
I do not wish to mock at these Posidonian Stoics and
Hermetics and Gnostics and Neo-Pythagoreans. They
loved goodness, and their faith is strong and even
terrible. One feels rather inclined to bow down before
their altars and cry : *Magna est Delusio et praevalebit.*

Yet on the whole one rises from these books with the impression that all this allegory and mysticism is bad for men. It may make the emotions sensitive, it certainly weakens the understanding. And, of course, in this paper I have left out of account many of the grosser forms of superstition. In any consideration of the balance, they should not be forgotten.

If a reader of Proclus and the *Corpus Hermeticum* wants relief, he will find it, perhaps, best in the writings of a gentle old Epicurean who lived at Oenoanda in Cappadocia about A. D. 200. His name was Diogenes.[1] His works are preserved, in a fragmentary state, not on papyrus or parchment, but on the wall of a large portico where he engraved them for passers-by to read. He lived in a world of superstition and foolish terror, and he wrote up the great doctrines of Epicurus for the saving of mankind.

'Being brought by age to the sunset of my life, and expecting at any moment to take my departure from the world with a glad song for the fullness of my happiness, I have resolved, lest I be taken too soon, to give help to those of good temperament. If one person or two or three or four, or any small number you choose, were in distress, and I were summoned out to help one after another, I would do all in my power to give the best counsel to each. But now, as I have said, the most of men lie sick, as it were of a pestilence, in their false beliefs about the world, and the tale of them increases ; for by imitation they take the disease from one another, like sheep. And further it is only just to bring help to those who shall come after us—for

---

[1] Published in the Teubner series by William, 1907.

they too are ours, though they be yet unborn ; and love for man commands us also to help strangers who may pass by. Since therefore the good message of the Book has gone forth to many, I have resolved to make use of this wall and to set forth in public the medicine of the healing of mankind.'

The people of his time and neighbourhood seem to have fancied that the old man must have some bad motive. They understood mysteries and redemptions and revelations. They understood magic and curses. But they were puzzled, apparently, by this simple message, which only told them to use their reason, their courage, and their sympathy, and not to be afraid of death or of angry gods. The doctrine was condensed into four sentences of a concentrated eloquence that make a translator despair : [1] ' Nothing to fear in God : Nothing to feel in Death : Good can be attained : Evil can be endured.'

Of course, the doctrines of this good old man do not represent the whole truth. To be guided by one's aversions is always a sign of weakness or defeat ; and it is as much a failure of nerve to reject blindly for fear of being a fool, as to believe blindly for fear of missing some emotional stimulus.

There is no royal road in these matters. I confess it seems strange to me as I write here, to reflect that at this moment many of my friends and most of my

---

[1]   Ἄφοβον ὁ θεός. Ἀναίσθητον ὁ θάνατος.

Τὸ ἀγαθὸν εὔκτητον. Τὸ δεινὸν εὐεκκαρτέρητον.

I regret to say that I cannot track this Epicurean ' tetractys ' to its source.

fellow creatures are, as far as one can judge, quite
confident that they possess supernatural knowledge.
As a rule, each individual belongs to some body which
has received in writing the results of a divine revelation.
I cannot share in any such feeling. The Uncharted
surrounds us on every side and we must needs have
some relation towards it, a relation which will depend
on the general discipline of a man's mind and the bias
of his whole character. As far as knowledge and
conscious reason will go, we should follow resolutely
their austere guidance. When they cease, as cease they
must, we must use as best we can those fainter powers
of apprehension and surmise and sensitiveness by
which, after all, most high truth has been reached as
well as most high art and poetry : careful always really
to seek for truth and not for our own emotional
satisfaction, careful not to neglect the real needs of men
and women through basing our life on dreams ; and
remembering above all to walk gently in a world where
the lights are dim and the very stars wander.

BIBLIOGRAPHICAL NOTE

It is not my purpose to make anything like a systematic bibliography,
but a few recommendations may be useful to some students who
approach this subject, as I have done, from the side of classical Greek.

For Greek Philosophy I have used besides Plato and Aristotle,
Diogenes Laertius and Philodemus, Diels, *Fragmente der Vorsokratiker* ;
Diels, *Doxographi Graeci* ; von Arnim, *Stoicorum Veterum Fragmenta* ;
Usener, *Epicurea* ; also the old *Fragmenta Philosophorum* of Mullach.

For later Paganism and Gnosticism, Reitzenstein, *Poimandres* ;
Reitzenstein, *Die hellenistischen Mysterienreligionen* ; Dieterich, *Eine
Mithrasliturgie* (also *Abraxas, Nekyia, Muttererde,* &c.) ; P. Wend-

land, *Hellenistisch-Römische Kultur*; Cumont, *Textes et Monuments relatifs aux Mystères de Mithra* (also *The Mysteries of Mithra*, Chicago, 1903), and *Les Religions Orientales dans l'Empire Romain*; Seeck, *Untergang der antiken Welt*, vol. iii; Philo, *de Vita Contemplativa*, Conybeare; Gruppe, *Griechische Religion und Mythologie*, pp. 1458–1676; Bousset, *Hauptprobleme der Gnosis*, 1907, with good bibliography in the introduction; articles by E. Bevan in the *Quarterly Review*, No. 424 (June 1910), and the *Hibbert Journal*, xi. 1 (October 1912). *Dokumente der Gnosis*, by W. Schultz (Jena, 1910), gives a highly subjective translation and reconstruction of most of the Gnostic documents: the *Corpus Hermeticum* is translated into English by G. R. S. Meade, *Thrice Greatest Hermes*, 1906. The first volume of Dr. Scott's monumental edition of the *Hermetica* (Clarendon Press, 1924) has appeared just too late to be used in the present volume.

For Jewish thought before the Christian era Dr. Charles's *Testaments of the Twelve Patriarchs*; also the same writer's *Book of Enoch*, and the *Religionsgeschichtliche Erklärung des Neuen Testaments* by Carl Clemen, Giessen, 1909.

Of Christian writers apart from the New Testament those that come most into account are Hippolytus († A. D. 250), *Refutatio Omnium Haeresium*, Epiphanius (367–403), *Panarion*, and Irenaeus († A. D. 202), *Contra Haereses*, i, ii. For a simple introduction to the problems presented by the New Testament literature I would venture to recommend Prof. Bacon's *New Testament*, in the Home University Library, and Dr. Estlin Carpenter's *First Three Gospels*. In such a vast literature I dare not make any further recommendations, but for a general introduction to the History of Religions with a good and brief bibliography I would refer the reader to Salomon Reinach's *Orpheus* (Paris, 1909; English translation the same year), a book of wide learning and vigorous thought.

V

THE LAST PROTEST

V

THE LAST PROTEST

In the last essay we have followed Greek popular religion to the very threshold of Christianity, till we found not only a soil ready for the seed of Christian metaphysic, but a large number of the plants already in full and exuberant growth. A complete history of Greek religion ought, without doubt, to include at least the rise of Christianity and the growth of the Orthodox Church, but, of course, the present series of studies does not aim at completeness. We will take the Christian theology for granted as we took the classical Greek philosophy, and will finish with a brief glance at the Pagan reaction of the fourth century, when the old religion, already full of allegory, mysticism, asceticism, and Oriental influences, raised itself for a last indignant stand against the all-prevailing deniers of the gods.

This period, however, admits a rather simpler treatment than the others. It so happens that for the last period of paganism we actually possess an authoritative statement of doctrine, something between a creed and a catechism. It seems to me a document so singularly important and, as far as I can make out, so little known, that I shall venture to print it entire.

A creed or catechism is, of course, not at all the same thing as the real religion of those who subscribe to it. The rules of metre are not the same thing as poetry ; the rules of cricket, if the analogy may be excused, are not the same thing as good play. Nay, more. A man states in his creed only the articles which he thinks it right to assert positively against those who think otherwise. His deepest and most practical beliefs are those on which he acts without question, which have never occurred to him as being open to doubt. If you take on the one hand a number of persons who have accepted the same creed but lived in markedly different ages and societies, with markedly different standards of thought and conduct, and on the other an equal number who profess different creeds but live in the same general environment, I think there will probably be more real identity of religion in the latter group. Take three orthodox Christians, enlightened according to the standards of their time, in the fourth, the sixteenth, and the twentieth centuries respectively, I think you will find more profound differences of religion between them than between a Methodist, a Catholic, a Freethinker, and even perhaps a well-educated Buddhist or Brahmin at the present day, provided you take the most generally enlightened representatives of each class. Still, when a student is trying to understand the inner religion of the ancients, he realizes how immensely valuable a creed or even a regular liturgy would be.

Literature enables us sometimes to approach pretty close, in various ways, to the minds of certain of the

great men of antiquity, and understand how they
thought and felt about a good many subjects. At
times one of these subjects is the accepted religion of
their society ; we can see how they criticized it or
rejected it. But it is very hard to know from their
reactions against it what that accepted religion really
was. Who, for instance, knows Herodotus's religion ?
He talks in his penetrating and garrulous way, 'sometimes for children and sometimes for philosophers,' as
Gibbon puts it, about everything in the world ; but
at the end of his book you find that he has not opened
his heart on this subject. No doubt his profession
as a reciter and story-teller prevented him. We can
see that Thucydides was sceptical ; but can we fully
see what his scepticism was directed against, or where,
for instance, Nikias would have disagreed with him,
and where he and Nikias both agreed against us ?

We have, of course, the systems of the great philosophers—especially of Plato and Aristotle. Better than
either, perhaps, we can make out the religion of
M. Aurelius. Amid all the harshness and plainness
of his literary style, Marcus possessed a gift which has
been granted to few, the power of writing down what
was in his heart just as it was, not obscured by
any consciousness of the presence of witnesses or any
striving after effect. He does not seem to have tried
deliberately to reveal himself, yet he has revealed
himself in that short personal note-book almost as
much as the great inspired egotists, Rousseau and
St. Augustine. True, there are some passages in
the book which are unintelligible to us ; that is

natural in a work which was not meant to be read by the public; broken flames of the white passion that consumed him bursting through the armour of his habitual accuracy and self-restraint.

People fail to understand Marcus, not because of his lack of self-expression, but because it is hard for most men to breathe at that intense height of spiritual life, or, at least, to breathe soberly. They can do it if they are allowed to abandon themselves to floods of emotion, and to lose self-judgement and self-control. I am often rather surprised at good critics speaking of Marcus as ' cold '. There is as much intensity of feeling in Tὰ εἰς ἑαυτόν as in most of the nobler modern books of religion, only there is a sterner power controlling it. The feeling never amounts to complete self-abandonment. ' The Guiding Power ' never trembles upon its throne, and the emotion is severely purged of earthly dross. That being so, we children of earth respond to it less readily.

Still, whether or no we can share Marcus's religion, we can at any rate understand most of it. But even then we reach only the personal religion of a very extraordinary man; we are not much nearer to the religion of the average educated person—the background against which Marcus, like Plato, ought to stand out. I believe that our conceptions of it are really very vague and various. Our great-grandfathers who read ' Tully's *Offices* and *Ends* ' were better informed than we. But there are many large and apparently simple questions about which, even after reading Cicero's philosophical translations, scholars probably feel quite uncertain. Were the morals of Epictetus or the morals of Part V of the Anthology most near to those of real life among respectable persons? Are there not subjects on which Plato himself sometimes makes our flesh creep? What are we to feel about slavery, about the exposing of children? True, slavery was not peculiar to antiquity ; it flourished in a civilized and peculiarly humane people of English blood till a generation ago. And the history of infanticide among the finest modern nations is such as to make one reluctant to throw stones, and even doubtful in which direction to throw them. Still, these great facts and others like them have to be understood, and are rather hard to understand, in their bearing on the religious life of the ancients.

Points of minor morals again are apt to surprise a reader of ancient literature. We must remember, of course, that they always do surprise one, in every age of history, as soon as its manners are studied in detail. One need not go beyond Salimbene's Chronicle, one need hardly go beyond Macaulay's History, or any of the famous French memoirs, to realize that. Was it really an ordinary thing in the first century, as Philo seems to say, for gentlemen at dinner-parties to black one another's eyes or bite one another's ears off? [1] Or were such practices confined to some Smart Set? Or was Philo, for his own purposes, using some particular scandalous occurrence as if it was typical?

St. Augustine mentions among the virtues of his

---

[1] *De Vit. Contempl.*, p. 477 M.

mother her unusual meekness and tact. Although her
husband had a fiery temper, she never had bruises on
her face, which made her a *rara avis* among the matrons
of her circle.[1] Her circle, presumably, included
Christians as well as Pagans and Manicheans. And
Philo's circle can scarcely be considered Pagan. Indeed,
as for the difference of religion, we should bear in mind
that, just at the time we are about to consider, the
middle of the fourth century, the conduct of the
Christians, either to the rest of the world or to one
another, was very far from evangelical. Ammianus
says that no savage beasts could equal its cruelty;
Ammianus was a pagan; but St. Gregory himself says
it was like Hell.[2]

I have expressed elsewhere my own general answer
to this puzzle.[3] Not only in early Greek times, but
throughout the whole of antiquity the possibility of all
sorts of absurd and atrocious things lay much nearer,
the protective forces of society were much weaker, the
strain on personal character, the need for real ' wisdom
and virtue ', was much greater than it is at the present
day. That is one of the causes that make antiquity so
interesting. Of course, different periods of antiquity
varied greatly, both in the conventional standard
demanded and in the spiritual force which answered
or surpassed the demand. But, in general, the strong
governments and orderly societies of modern Europe
have made it infinitely easier for men of no particular
virtue to live a decent life, infinitely easier also for

---

[1] *Conf.* ix. 9.   [2] Gibbon, chap. xxi, notes 161, 162.
[3] *Rise of the Greek Epic*, chap. i.

men of no particular reasoning power or scientific knowledge to have a more or less scientific or sane view of the world.

That, however, does not carry us far towards solving the main problem : it brings us no nearer to knowledge of anything that we may call typically a religious creed or an authorized code of morals, in any age from Hesiod to M. Aurelius.

The book which I have ventured to call a Creed or Catechism is the work of Sallustius *About the Gods and the World*, a book, I should say, about the length of the Scottish Shorter Catechism. It is printed in the third volume of Mullach's *Fragmenta Philosophorum* ; apart from that, the only edition generally accessible—and that is rare—is a duodecimo published by Allatius in 1539. Orelli's brochure of 1821 seems to be unprocurable.

The author was in all probability that Sallustius who is known to us as a close friend of Julian before his accession, and a backer or inspirer of the emperor's efforts to restore the old religion. He was concerned in an educational edition of Sophocles—the seven selected plays now extant with a commentary. He was given the rank of prefect in 362, that of consul in 363. One must remember, of course, that in that rigorous and ascetic court high rank connoted no pomp or luxury. Julian had dismissed the thousand hairdressers, the innumerable cooks and eunuchs of his Christian predecessor. It probably brought with it only an increased obligation to live on pulse and to do without such pamperings of the body as fine clothes or warmth or washing.

Julian's fourth oration, a prose hymn *To King Sun*, πρὸς Ἥλιον βασιλέα, is dedicated to Sallustius; his eighth is a 'Consolation to Himself upon the Departure of Sallustius '. (He had been with Julian in the wars in Gaul, and was recalled by the jealousy of the emperor Constantius.) It is a touching and even a noble treatise. The nervous self-distrust which was habitual in Julian makes him write always with a certain affectation, but no one could mistake the real feeling of loss and loneliness that runs through the consolation. He has lost his ' comrade in the ranks ', and now is ' Odysseus left alone '. So he writes, quoting the *Iliad*; Sallustius has been carried by God outside the spears and arrows : ' which malignant men were always aiming at you, or rather at me, trying to wound me through you, and believing that the only way to beat me down was by depriving me of the fellowship of my true friend and fellow-soldier, the comrade who never flinched from sharing my dangers.'

One note recurs four times ; he has lost the one man to whom he could talk as a brother ; the man of ' guileless and clean free-speech ',[1] who was honest and unafraid and able to contradict the emperor freely because of their mutual trust. If one thinks of it, Julian, for all his gentleness, must have been an alarming emperor to converse with. His standard of conduct was not only uncomfortably high, it was also a little unaccountable. The most correct and blameless court

---

[1] ἄδολος καὶ καθαρὰ παρρησία.

officials must often have suspected that their master
looked upon them as simply wallowing in sin. And that
feeling does not promote ease or truthfulness. Julian
compares his friendship with Sallustius to that of Scipio
and Laelius. People said of Scipio that he only carried
out what Laelius told him. ' Is that true of me ? '
Julian asks himself. ' Have I only done what Sallustius
told me ? ' His answer is sincere and beautiful : κοινὰ
τὰ φίλων. It little matters who suggested, and who
agreed to the suggestion ; his thoughts, and any credit
that came from the thoughts, are his friend's as much
as his own. We happen to hear from the Christian
Theodoret (*Hist.* iii. 11) that on one occasion when
Julian was nearly goaded into persecution of the
Christians, it was Sallustius who recalled him to their
fixed policy of toleration.

Sallustius then may be taken to represent in the
most authoritative way the Pagan reaction of Julian's
time, in its final struggle against Christianity.

He was, roughly speaking, a Neo-Platonist. But it is
not as a professed philosopher that he writes. It is only
that Neo-Platonism had permeated the whole atmosphere of the age.[1] The strife of the philosophical
sects had almost ceased. Just as Julian's mysticism
made all gods and almost all forms of worship into
one, so his enthusiasm for Hellenism revered, nay,

[1] ' Many of his sections come straight from Plotinus : xiv and xv
perhaps from Porphyry's *Letter to Marcella*, an invaluable document
for the religious side of Neo-Platonism. A few things (prayer to the
souls of the dead in iv, to the Cosmos in xvii, the doctrine of τύχη in ix)
are definitely un-Plotinian : probably concessions to popular religion.'
—E. R. D.

idolized, almost all the great philosophers of the past.
They were all trying to say the same ineffable thing ;
all lifting mankind towards the knowledge of God.
I say ' almost ' in both cases ; for the Christians are
outside the pale in one domain and the Epicureans
and a few Cynics in the other. Both had committed
the cardinal sin ; they had denied the gods. They
are sometimes lumped together as *Atheoi. L'athéisme,
voilà l'ennemi.*

This may surprise us at first sight, but the explanation is easy. To Julian the one great truth that
matters is the presence and glory of the gods. No
doubt, they are all ultimately one ; they are δυνάμεις,
' forces,' not persons, but for reasons above our comprehension they are manifest only under conditions
of form, time, and personality, and have so been
revealed and worshipped and partly known by the
great minds of the past. In Julian's mind the religious
emotion itself becomes the thing to live for. Every
object that has been touched by that emotion is thereby
glorified and made sacred. Every shrine where men
have worshipped in truth of heart is thereby a house of
God. The worship may be mixed up with all sorts of
folly, all sorts of unedifying practice. Such things
must be purged away, or, still better, must be properly
understood. For to the pure all things are pure ; and
the myths that shock the vulgar are noble allegories to
the wise and reverent. Purge religion from dross, if
you like ; but remember that you do so at your peril.
One false step, one self-confident rejection of a thing
which is merely too high for you to grasp, and you are

darkening the Sun, casting God out of the world.
And that was just what the Christians deliberately
did. In many of the early Christian writings denial
is a much greater element than assertion. The beautiful *Octavius* of Minucius Felix (about A. D. 130–60)
is an example. Such denial was, of course, to our
judgement, eminently needed, and rendered a great
service to the world. But to Julian it seemed impiety.
In other Christian writings the misrepresentation of
pagan rites and beliefs is decidedly foul-mouthed and
malicious. Quite apart from his personal wrongs and
his contempt for the character of Constantius, Julian
could have no sympathy for men who overturned altars
and heaped blasphemy on old deserted shrines, defilers
of every sacred object that was not protected by
popularity. The most that such people could expect
from him was that they should not be proscribed
by law.

But meantime what were the multitudes of the
god-fearing to believe? The arm of the state was not
very strong or effective. Labour as he might to
supply good teaching to all provincial towns, Julian
could not hope to educate the poor and ignorant to
understand Plato and M. Aurelius. For them, he
seems to say, all that is necessary is that they should
be pious and god-fearing in their own way. But for
more or less educated people, not blankly ignorant, and
yet not professed students of philosophy, there might
be some simple and authoritative treatise issued—
a sort of reasoned creed, to lay down in a convincing
manner the outlines of the old Hellenic religion, before

the Christians and Atheists should have swept all fear
of the gods from off the earth.

The treatise is this work of Sallustius.

The Christian fathers from Minucius Felix onward
have shown us what was the most vulnerable point of
Paganism : the traditional mythology. Sallustius deals
with it at once. The *Akroâtês*, or pupil, he says in
Section 1, needs some preliminary training. He should
have been well brought up, should not be incurably
stupid, and should not have been familiarized with
foolish fables. Evidently the mythology was not to
be taught to children. He enunciates certain postulates of religious thought, viz. that God is always good
and not subject to passion or to change, and then
proceeds straight to the traditional myths. In the
first place, he insists that they are what he calls
' divine '. That is, they are inspired or have some
touch of divine truth in them. This is proved by
the fact that they have been uttered, and sometimes
invented, by the most inspired poets and philosophers
and by the gods themselves in oracles—a very characteristic argument.

The myths are all expressions of God and of the
goodness of God ; but they follow the usual method
of divine revelation, to wit, mystery and allegory.
The myths state clearly the one tremendous fact that
the Gods *are* ; that is what Julian cared about and
the Christians denied : *what* they are the myths
reveal only to those who have understanding. ' The
world itself is a great myth, in which bodies and

inanimate things are visible, souls and minds invisible.'

'But, admitting all this, how comes it that the myths are so often absurd and even immoral?' For the usual purpose of mystery and allegory; in order to make people think. The soul that wishes to know God must make its own effort; it cannot expect simply to lie still and be told. The myths by their obvious falsity and absurdity on the surface stimulate the mind capable of religion to probe deeper.

He proceeds to give instances, and chooses at once myths that had been for generations the mock of the sceptic, and in his own day furnished abundant ammunition for the artillery of Christian polemic. He takes first Hesiod's story of Kronos swallowing his children; then the Judgement of Paris; then comes a long and earnest explanation of the myth of Attis and the Mother of the Gods. It is on the face of it a story highly discreditable both to the heart and the head of those august beings, and though the rites themselves do not seem to have been in any way improper, the Christians naturally attacked the Pagans and Julian personally for countenancing the worship. Sallustius's explanation is taken directly from Julian's fifth oration in praise of the Great Mother, and reduces the myth and the ritual to an expression of the adventures of the Soul seeking God.

So much for the whole traditional mythology. It has been explained completely away and made subservient to philosophy and edification, while it can

still be used as a great well-spring of religious emotion.
For the explanations given by Sallustius and Julian are
never rationalistic. They never stimulate a spirit of
scepticism, always a spirit of mysticism and reverence.
And, lest by chance even this reverent theorizing
should have been somehow lacking in insight or true
piety, Sallustius ends with the prayer : ' When I say
these things concerning the myths, may the gods
themselves and the spirits of those who wrote the
myths be gracious to me.'

He now leaves mythology and turns to the First
Cause. It must be one, and it must be present in all
things. Thus, it cannot be Life, for, if it were, all things
would be alive. By a Platonic argument in which
he will still find some philosophers to follow him, he
proves that everything which exists, exists because of
some goodness in it ; and thus arrives at the conclusion
that the First Cause is τὸ ἀγαθόν, the Good.

The gods are emanations or forces issuing from the
Good ; the makers of this world are secondary gods ;
above them are the makers of the makers, above all
the One.

Next comes a proof that the world is eternal—a very
important point of doctrine ; next that the soul is
immortal ; next a definition of the workings of Divine
Providence, Fate, and Fortune—a fairly skilful piece
of dialectic dealing with a hopeless difficulty. Next
come Virtue and Vice, and, in a dead and perfunctory
echo of Plato's *Republic*, an enumeration of the good
and bad forms of human society. The questions which
vibrated with life in free Athens had become meaning-

less to a despot-governed world. Then follows more adventurous matter.

First a chapter headed : ' Whence Evil things come, and that there is no *Phusis Kakou*—Evil is not a real thing.' ' It is perhaps best ', he says, ' to observe at once that, since the gods are good and make everything, there is no positive evil ; there is only absence of good ; just as there is no positive darkness, only absence of light.'

What we call ' evils ' arise only in the activities of men, and even here no one ever does evil for the sake of evil. ' One who indulges in some pleasant vice thinks the vice bad but his pleasure good ; a murderer thinks the murder bad, but the money he will get by it, good ; one who injures an enemy thinks the injury bad, but the being quits with his enemy, good ' ; and so on. The evil acts are all done for the sake of some good, but human souls, being very far removed from the original flawless divine nature, make mistakes or sins. One of the great objects of the world, he goes on to explain, of gods, men, and spirits, of religious institutions and human laws alike, is to keep the souls from these errors and to purge them again when they have fallen.

Next comes a speculative difficulty. Sallustius has called the world ' eternal in the fullest sense '—that is, it always has been and always will be. And yet it is ' made ' by the gods. How are these statements compatible ? If it was made, there must have been a time before it was made. The answer is ingenious. It is not made by handicraft as a table is ; it is not begotten as a son by a father. It is the result of a quality of God just as light is the result of a quality of the sun. The sun causes light, but the light is there as soon as the sun is there. The world is simply the other side, as it were, of the goodness of God, and has existed as long as that goodness has existed.

Next come some simpler questions about man's relation to the gods. In what sense can we say that the gods are angry with the wicked or are appeased by repentance? Sallustius is quite firm. The gods cannot ever be glad—for that which is glad is also sorry ; cannot be angry—for anger is a passion ; and obviously they cannot be appeased by gifts or prayers. Even men, if they are honest, require higher motives than that. God is unchangeable, always good, always doing good. If we are good, we are nearer to the gods, and we feel it ; if we are evil, we are separated further from them. It is not they that are angry, it is our sins that hide them from us and prevent the goodness of God from shining into us. If we repent, again, we do not make any change in God ; we only, by the conversion of our soul towards the divine, heal our own badness and enjoy again the goodness of the gods. To say that the gods turn away from the wicked, would be like saying that the sun turns away from a blind man.

Why then do we make offerings and sacrifices to the gods, when the gods need nothing and can have nothing added to them? We do so in order to have more communion with the gods. The whole temple service, in fact, is an elaborate allegory, a representation of the divine government of the world.

The custom of sacrificing animals had died out some time before this. The Jews of the Dispersion had

given it up long since because the Law forbade any
such sacrifice outside the Temple.[1] When Jerusalem
was destroyed Jewish sacrifice ceased altogether. The
Christians seem from the beginning to have generally
followed the Jewish practice. But sacrifice was in
itself not likely to continue in a society of large towns.
It meant turning your temples into very ill-conducted
slaughter-houses, and was also associated with a great
deal of muddled and indiscriminate charity.[2] One
might have hoped that men so high-minded and
spiritual as Julian and Sallustius would have considered
this practice unnecessary or even have reformed it
away. But no. It was part of the genuine Hellenic
tradition ; and no jot or tittle of that tradition should,
if they could help it, be allowed to die. Sacrifice is
desirable, argues Sallustius, because it is a gift of life.
God has given us life, as He has given us all else. We
must therefore pay to Him some emblematic tithe of
life. Again, prayers in themselves are merely words ;
but with sacrifice they are words plus life, Living
Words. Lastly, we are Life of a sort, and God is Life
of an infinitely higher sort. To approach Him we need
always a medium or a mediator ; the medium between
life and life must needs be life. We find that life in the
sacrificed animal.[3]

[1] S. Reinach, *Orpheus*, p. 273 (Engl. trans., p. 185).

[2] See Ammianus, xxii. 12, on the bad effect of Julian's sacrifices.
Sacrifice was finally forbidden by the emperor Theodosius in 391. It
was condemned by Theophrastus, and is said by Porphyry (*De Abstinen-
tia*, ii. 11) simply λαβεῖν τὴν ἀρχὴν ἐξ ἀδικίας.

[3] Sallustius's view of sacrifice is curiously like the illuminating

The argument shows what ingenuity these religious men had at their command, and what trouble they would take to avoid having to face a fact and reform a bad system.

There follows a long and rather difficult argument to show that the world is, in itself, eternal. The former discussion on this point had only shown that the gods would not destroy it. This shows that its own nature is indestructible. The arguments are very inconclusive, though clever, and one wonders why the author is at so much pains. Indeed, he is so earnest that at the end of the chapter he finds it necessary to apologize to the Kosmos in case his language should have been indiscreet. The reason, I think, is that the Christians were still, as in apostolic times, pinning their faith to the approaching end of the world by fire.[1] They announced the end of the world as near, and they rejoiced in the prospect of its destruction. History has shown more than once what terrible results can be produced by such beliefs as these in the minds of excitable and suffering popula-

---

theory of MM. Hubert and Mauss, in which they define primitive sacrifice as a medium, a bridge or lightning-conductor, between the profane and the sacred. 'Essai sur la Nature et la Fonction du Sacrifice' (*Année Sociologique*, ii. 1897–8), since republished in the *Mélanges d'Histoire des Religions*, 1909.

[1] Cf. Minucius Felix, *Octavius*, p. 96, Ouzel (chap. 11, Boenig). 'Quid quod toti orbi et ipsi mundo cum sideribus suis minantur incendium, ruinam moliuntur?' The doctrine in their mouths became a very different thing from the Stoic theory of the periodic re-absorption of the universe in the Divine Element. Ibid., pp. 322 ff. (34 Boenig).

tions, especially those of eastern blood. It was widely
believed that Christian fanatics had from time to time
actually tried to light fires which should consume the
accursed world and thus hasten the coming of the
kingdom which should bring such incalculable rewards
to their own organization and plunge the rest of mankind in everlasting torment. To any respectable Pagan
such action was an insane crime made worse by a
diabolical motive. The destruction of the world,
therefore, seems to have become a subject of profound
irritation, if not actually of terror. At any rate the
doctrine lay at the very heart of the *perniciosa
superstitio*, and Sallustius uses his best dialectic
against it.

The title of Chapter XVIII has a somewhat pathetic
ring : ' Why are *Atheïai* '—Atheisms or rejections of
God—' permitted, and that God is not injured thereby.' Θεὸς οὐ βλάπτεται. ' If over certain parts of the
world there have occurred (and will occur more hereafter) rejections of the gods, a wise man need not be
disturbed at that.' We have always known that the
human soul was prone to error. God's providence is
there ; but we cannot expect all men at all times and
places to enjoy it equally. In the human body it is
only the eye that sees the light, the rest of the body is
ignorant of the light. So are many parts of the earth
ignorant of God.

Very likely, also, this rejection of God is a punishment. Persons who in a previous life have known the
gods but disregarded them, are perhaps now born, as it
were, blind, unable to see God ; persons who have

committed the blasphemy of worshipping their own
kings as gods may perhaps now be cast out from the
knowledge of God.

Philosophy had always rejected the Man-God,
especially in the form of King-worship; but opposition to Christianity no doubt intensifies the
protest.

The last chapter is very short. 'Souls that have
lived in virtue, being otherwise blessed and especially
separated from their irrational part and purged of all
body, are joined with the gods and sway the whole
world together with them.' So far triumphant faith :
then the after-thought of the brave man who means
to live his best life even if faith fail him. 'But even
if none of these rewards came to them, still Virtue
itself and the Joy and Glory of Virtue, and the Life
that is subject to no grief and no master, would be
enough to make blessed those who have set themselves
to live in Virtue and have succeeded.'

There the book ends. It ends upon that well-worn
paradox which, from the second book of the *Republic*
onwards, seems to have brought so much comfort to
the nobler spirits of the ancient world. Strange how
we moderns cannot rise to it ! We seem simply to lack
the intensity of moral enthusiasm. When we speak of
martyrs being happy on the rack ; in the first place we
rarely believe it, and in the second we are usually
supposing that the rack will soon be over and that harps
and golden crowns will presently follow. The ancient
moralist believed that the good man was happy then

and there, because the joy, being in his soul, was not affected by the torture of his body.[1]

Not being able fully to feel this conviction, we naturally incline to think it affected or unreal. But, taking the conditions of the ancient world into account, we must admit that the men who uttered this belief at least understood better than most of us what suffering was. Many of them were slaves, many had been captives of war. They knew what they were talking about. I think, on a careful study of M. Aurelius, Epictetus, and some of these Neo-Platonic philosophers, that we shall be forced to realize that these men could rise to much the same heights of religious heroism as the Catholic saints of the Middle Age, and that they often did so—if I may use such a phrase—on a purer and thinner diet of sensuous emotion, with less wallowing in the dust and less delirium.

Be that as it may, we have now seen in outline the kind of religion which ancient Paganism had become at the time of its final reaction against Christianity. It is a more or less intelligible whole, and succeeds better than most religions in combining two great appeals. It appeals to the philosopher and the thoughtful man as a fairly complete and rational system of thought, which speculative and enlightened minds in any age might believe without disgrace. I do not mean that it is probably true; to me all these overpowering optimisms which, by means of a few untested *a priori* postulates, affect triumphantly

---

[1] Even Epicurus himself held κἂν στρεβλωθῇ ὁ σοφός, εἶναι αὐτὸν εὐδαίμονα. Diog. La. x. 118. See above, end of chap. iii.

to disprove the most obvious facts of life, seem very soon to become meaningless. I conceive it to be no comfort at all, to a man suffering agonies of frost-bite, to be told by science that cold is merely negative and does not exist. So far as the statement is true it is irrelevant; so far as it pretends to be relevant it is false. I only mean that a system like that of Sallustius is, judged by any standard, high, civilized, and enlightened.

At the same time this religion appeals to the ignorant and the humble-minded. It takes from the pious villager no single object of worship that has turned his thoughts heavenwards. It may explain and purge; it never condemns or ridicules. In its own eyes that was its great glory, in the eyes of history perhaps its most fatal weakness. Christianity, apart from its positive doctrines, had inherited from Judaism the noble courage of its disbeliefs.

To compare this Paganism in detail with its great rival would be, even if I possessed the necessary learning, a laborious and unsatisfactory task. But if a student with very imperfect knowledge may venture a personal opinion on this obscure subject, it seems to me that we often look at such problems from a wrong angle. Harnack somewhere, in discussing the comparative success or failure of various early Christian sects, makes the illuminating remark that the main determining cause in each case was not their comparative reasonableness of doctrine or skill in controversy —for they practically never converted one another— but simply the comparative increase or decrease of the

birth-rate in the respective populations. On somewhat
similar lines it always appears to me that, historically
speaking, the character of Christianity in these early
centuries is to be sought not so much in the doctrines
which it professed, nearly all of which had their roots
and their close parallels in older Hellenistic or Hebrew
thought, but in the organization on which it rested.
For my own part, when I try to understand Christianity as a mass of doctrines, Gnostic, Trinitarian,
Monophysite, Arian and the rest, I get no further.
When I try to realize it as a sort of semi-secret society
for mutual help with a mystical religious basis, resting
first on the proletariates of Antioch and the great
commercial and manufacturing towns of the Levant,
then spreading by instinctive sympathy to similar classes
in Rome and the West, and rising in influence, like
certain other mystical cults, by the special appeal it
made to women, the various historical puzzles begin
to fall into place. Among other things this explains
the strange subterranean power by which the emperor
Diocletian was baffled, and to which the pretender
Constantine had to capitulate; it explains its
humanity, its intense feeling of brotherhood within its
own bounds, its incessant care for the poor, and also
its comparative indifference to the virtues which are
specially incumbent on a governing class, such as states-
manship, moderation, truthfulness, active courage,
learning, culture, and public spirit. Of course, such
indifference was only comparative. After the time of
Constantine the governing classes come into the fold,
bringing with them their normal qualities, and there-

after it is Paganism, not Christianity, that must uphold the flag of a desperate fidelity in the face of a hostile world—a task to which, naturally enough, Paganism was not equal. But I never wished to pit the two systems against one another. The battle is over, and it is poor work to jeer at the wounded and the dead. If we read the literature of the time, especially some records of the martyrs under Diocletian, we shall at first perhaps imagine that, apart from some startling exceptions, the conquered party were all vicious and hateful, the conquerors, all wise and saintly. Then, looking a little deeper, we shall see that this great controversy does not stand altogether by itself. As in other wars, each side had its wise men and its foolish, its good men and its evil. Like other conquerors these conquerors were often treacherous and brutal; like other vanquished these vanquished have been tried at the bar of history without benefit of counsel, have been condemned in their absence and died with their lips sealed. The polemic literature of Christianity is loud and triumphant, the books of the Pagans have been destroyed.

Only an ignorant man will pronounce a violent or bitter judgement here. The minds that are now tender, timid, and reverent in their orthodoxy would probably in the third or fourth century have sided with the old gods; those of more daring and puritan temper with the Christians. The historian will only try to have sympathy and understanding for both. They are all dead now, Diocletian and Ignatius, Cyril and Hypatia, Julian and Basil, Athanasius and

Arîus : every party has yielded up its persecutors and
its martyrs, its hates and slanders and aspirations and
heroisms, to the arms of that great Silence whose
secrets they all claimed so loudly to have read. Even
the dogmas for which they fought might seem to be
dead too. For if Julian and Sallustius, Gregory and
John Chrysostom, were to rise again and see the world
as it now is, they would probably feel their personal
differences melt away in comparison with the vast
difference between their world and this. They fought
to the death about this credo and that, but the same
spirit was in all of them. In the words of one who
speaks with greater knowledge than mine, ' the most
inward man in these four contemporaries is the same.
It is the Spirit of the Fourth Century.' [1]

'Dieselbe Seelenstimmung, derselbe Spiritualismus';
also the same passionate asceticism. All through
antiquity the fight against luxury was a fiercer and
stronger fight than comes into our modern experience.
There was not more objective luxury in any period of
ancient history than there is now ; there was never anything like so much. But there does seem to have been
more subjective abandonment to physical pleasure and
concomitantly a stronger protest against it. From
some time before the Christian era it seems as if the
subconscious instinct of humanity was slowly rousing
itself for a great revolt against the long intolerable
tyranny of the senses over the soul, and by the fourth
century the revolt threatened to become all-absorbing.

[1] Geffcken in the *Neue Jahrbücher*, xxi. 162 f.

The Emperor Julian was probably as proud of his fireless cell and the crowding lice in his beard and cassock as an average Egyptian monk. The ascetic movement grew, as we all know, to be measureless and insane. It seemed to be almost another form of lust, and to have the same affinities with cruelty. But it has probably rendered priceless help to us who come afterwards. The insane ages have often done service for the sane, the harsh and suffering ages for the gentle and well-to-do.

Sophrosynê, however we try to translate it, temperance, gentleness, the spirit that in any trouble thinks and is patient, that saves and not destroys, is the right spirit. And it is to be feared that none of these fourth-century leaders, neither the fierce bishops with their homilies on Charity, nor Julian and Sallustius with their worship of Hellenism, came very near to that classic ideal. To bring back that note of Sophrosynê I will venture, before proceeding to the fourth-century Pagan creed, to give some sentences from an earlier Pagan prayer. It is cited by Stobaeus from a certain Eusebius, a late Ionic Platonist of whom almost nothing is known, not even the date at which he lived.[1] But the voice sounds like that of a stronger and more sober age.

' May I be no man's enemy,' it begins, ' and may I be the friend of that which is eternal and abides. May I never quarrel with those nearest to me ; and if I do, may I be reconciled quickly. May I never devise evil against any man ; if any devise evil against me, may I escape uninjured and without the need of

---

[1] Mullach, *Fragmenta Philosophorum*, iii. 7, from Stob. *Flor.* i. 85.

hurting him. May I love, seek, and attain only that which is good. May I wish for all men's happiness and envy none. May I never rejoice in the ill-fortune of one who has wronged me. . . . When I have done or said what is wrong, may I never wait for the rebuke of others, but always rebuke myself until I make amends. . . . May I win no victory that harms either me or my opponent. . . . May I reconcile friends who are wroth with one another. May I, to the extent of my power, give all needful help to my friends and to all who are in want. May I never fail a friend in danger. When visiting those in grief may I be able by gentle and healing words to soften their pain. . . . May I respect myself. . . . May I always keep tame that which rages within me. . . . May I accustom myself to be gentle, and never be angry with people because of circumstances. May I never discuss who is wicked and what wicked things he has done, but know good men and follow in their footsteps.'

There is more of it. How unpretending it is and yet how searching! And in the whole there is no petition for any material blessing, and—most striking of all—it is addressed to no personal god. It is pure prayer. Of course, to some it will feel thin and cold. Most men demand of their religion more outward and personal help, more physical ecstasy, a more heady atmosphere of illusion. No one man's attitude towards the Uncharted can be quite the same as his neighbour's. In part instinctively, in part superficially and self-consciously, each generation of mankind reacts against the last. The grown man turns from the lights that were thrust upon his eyes in childhood. The son shrugs his shoulders at the watchwords that thrilled his father, and with varying degrees of sensitiveness or dullness, of fuller or more fragmentary experience, writes out for himself the manuscript of his creed. Yet, even for the wildest or bravest rebel, that manuscript is only a palimpsest. On the surface all is new writing, clean and self-assertive. Underneath, dim but indelible in the very fibres of the parchment, lie the characters of many ancient aspirations and raptures and battles which his conscious mind has rejected or utterly forgotten. And forgotten things, if there be real life in them, will sometimes return out of the dust, vivid to help still in the forward groping of humanity. A religious system like that of Eusebius or Marcus, or even Sallustius, was not built up without much noble life and strenuous thought and a steady passion for the knowledge of God. Things of that make do not, as a rule, die for ever.

SALLUSTIUS

'ON THE GODS AND THE WORLD'

SALLUSTIUS

'ON THE GODS AND THE WORLD'[1]

I. *What the Disciple should be ; and concerning Common Conceptions.*

THOSE who wish to hear about the Gods should have been well guided from childhood, and not habituated to foolish beliefs. They should also be in disposition good and sensible, that they may properly attend to the teaching.

They ought also to know the Common Conceptions. Common Conceptions are those to which all men agree as soon as they are asked; for instance, that all God is good, free from passion, free from change. For whatever suffers change does so for the worse or the better: if for the worse, it is made bad; if for the better, it must have been bad at first.

II. *That God is unchanging, unbegotten, eternal, incorporeal, and not in space.*

Let the disciple be thus. Let the teachings be of the following sort. The essences of the Gods never

---

[1] I translate κόσμος generally as 'World', sometimes as 'Cosmos'. It always has the connotation of 'divine order'; ψυχή always 'Soul', to keep it distinct from ζωή, 'physical life', though often 'Life' would be a more natural English equivalent; ἐμψυχοῦν 'to animate'; οὐσία sometimes 'essence', sometimes 'being' (never 'substance' or 'nature'); φύσις 'nature'; σῶμα sometimes 'body', sometimes 'matter'.

came into existence (for that which always is never comes into existence; and that exists for ever which possesses primary force and by nature suffers nothing): neither do they consist of bodies; for even in bodies the powers are incorporeal. Neither are they contained by space; for that is a property of bodies. Neither are they separate from the First Cause nor from one another, just as thoughts are not separate from mind nor acts of knowledge from the soul.

III. *Concerning myths; that they are divine, and why.*

We may well inquire, then, why the ancients forsook these doctrines and made use of myths. There is this first benefit from myths, that we have to search and do not have our minds idle.

That the myths are divine can be seen from those who have used them. Myths have been used by inspired poets, by the best of philosophers, by those who established the mysteries, and by the Gods themselves in oracles. But *why* the myths are divine it is the duty of Philosophy to inquire. Since all existing things rejoice in that which is like them and reject that which is unlike, the stories about the Gods ought to be like the Gods, so that they may both be worthy of the divine essence and make the Gods well disposed to those who speak of them: which could only be done by means of myths.

Now the myths represent the Gods themselves and the goodness of the Gods—subject always to the distinction of the speakable and the unspeakable, the revealed and the unrevealed, that which is clear and that which is hidden : since, just as the Gods have made the goods of sense common to all, but those of intellect only to the wise, so the myths state the existence of Gods to all, but who and what they are only to those who can understand.

They also represent the activities of the Gods. For one may call the World a Myth, in which bodies and things are visible, but souls and minds hidden. Besides, to wish to teach the whole truth about the Gods to all produces contempt in the foolish, because they cannot understand, and lack of zeal in the good ; whereas to conceal the truth by myths prevents the contempt of the foolish, and compels the good to practise philosophy.

But why have they put in the myths stories of adultery, robbery, father-binding, and all the other absurdity? Is not that perhaps a thing worthy of admiration, done so that by means of the visible absurdity the Soul may immediately feel that the words are veils and believe the truth to be a mystery?

IV. *That the species of Myth are five, with examples of each.*

Of myths some are theological, some physical, some psychic, and again some material, and some mixed from these last two. The theological are those myths which use no bodily form but contemplate the very essences of the Gods : e. g. Kronos swallowing his children. Since God is intellectual, and all intellect returns

into itself, this myth expresses in allegory the essence
of God.

Myths may be regarded physically when they express
the activities of the Gods in the world : e. g. people
before now have regarded Kronos as Time, and calling
the divisions of Time his sons say that the sons are
swallowed by the father.

The psychic way is to regard the activities of the
Soul itself : the Soul's acts of thought, though they
pass on to other objects, nevertheless remain inside
their begetters.

The material and last is that which the Egyptians
have mostly used, owing to their ignorance, believing
material objects actually to be Gods, and so calling
them : e. g. they call the Earth Isis, moisture Osiris,
heat Typhon, or again, water Kronos, the fruits of the
earth Adonis, and wine Dionysus.

To say that these objects are sacred to the Gods,
like various herbs and stones and animals, is possible to
sensible men, but to say that they are gods is the
notion of madmen—except, perhaps, in the sense in
which both the orb of the sun and the ray which comes
from the orb are colloquially called ' the Sun '.[1]

The mixed kind of myth may be seen in many

[1] e. g. when we say ' The sun is coming in through the window ',
or in Greek ἐξαίφνης ἥκων ἐκ τοῦ ἡλίου, Plat. *Rep.* 516 E. This appears
to mean that you can loosely apply the term ' Osiris ' both to (i) the
real Osiris and (ii) the corn which comes from him, as you can apply
the name ' Sun ' both to (i) the real orb and (ii) the ray that comes
from the orb. However, Julian, *Or.* v, on the Sun suggests a different
view—that both the orb and the ray are mere effects and symbols of
the true spiritual Sun, as corn is of Osiris.

instances : for example they say that in a banquet of the Gods Discord threw down a golden apple ; the goddesses contended for it, and were sent by Zeus to Paris to be judged ; Paris saw Aphrodite to be beautiful and gave her the apple. Here the banquet signifies the hyper-cosmic powers of the Gods ; that is why they are all together. The golden apple is the world, which, being formed out of opposites, is naturally said to be ' thrown by Discord '. The different Gods bestow different gifts upon the world and are thus said to ' contend for the apple '. And the soul which lives according to sense—for that is what Paris is—not seeing the other powers in the world but only beauty, declares that the apple belongs to Aphrodite.

Theological myths suit philosophers, physical and psychic suit poets, mixed suit religious initiations, since every initiation aims at uniting us with the World and the Gods.

To take another myth, they say that the Mother of the Gods seeing Attis lying by the river Gallus fell in love with him, took him, crowned him with her cap of stars, and thereafter kept him with her. He fell in love with a nymph and left the Mother to live with her. For this the Mother of the Gods made Attis go mad and cut off his genital organs and leave them with the Nymph, and then return and dwell with her.

Now the Mother of the Gods is the principle that generates life ; that is why she is called Mother. Attis is the creator of all things which are born and die ; that is why he is said to have been found by the river

Gallus. For Gallus signifies the Galaxy, or Milky Way, the point at which body subject to passion begins.[1] Now as the primary gods make perfect the secondary, the Mother loves Attis and gives him celestial powers. That is what the cap means. Attis loves a nymph : the nymphs preside over generation, since all that is generated is fluid. But since the process of generation must be stopped somewhere, and not allowed to generate something worse than the worst, the Creator who makes these things casts away his generative powers into the creation and is joined to the gods again. Now these things never happened, but always are. And Mind sees all things at once, but Reason (or Speech) expresses some first and others after. Thus, as the myth is in accord with the Cosmos, we for that reason keep a festival imitating the Cosmos, for how could we attain higher order ?

And at first we ourselves, having fallen from heaven and living with the Nymph, are in despondency, and abstain from corn and all rich and unclean food, for both are hostile to the soul. Then comes the cutting of the tree and the fast, as though we also were cutting off the further process of generation. After that the feeding on milk, as though we were being born again ; after which come rejoicings and garlands and, as it were, a return up to the Gods.

The season of the ritual is evidence to the truth of these explanations. The rites are performed about

---

[1] ἄρχεσθαι Mr. L. W. Hunter, ἔρχεσθαι MS. Above the Milky Way there is no such body, only σῶμα ἀπαθές. Cf. Macrob. in *Somn. Scip.* i. 12.

the Vernal Equinox, when the fruits of the earth are ceasing to be produced, and day is becoming longer than night, which applies well to Spirits rising higher. (At least, the other equinox is in mythology the time of the Rape of Korê, which is the descent of the souls.)

May these explanations of the myths find favour in the eyes of the Gods themselves and the souls of those who wrote the myths.

V. *On the First Cause.*

Next in order comes knowledge of the First Cause and the subsequent orders of the gods, then the nature of the world, the essence of intellect and of soul, then Providence, Fate, and Fortune, then to see Virtue and Vice and the various forms of social constitution good and bad that are formed from them, and from what possible source Evil came into the world.

Each of these subjects needs many long discussions ; but there is perhaps no harm in stating them briefly, so that a disciple may not be completely ignorant about them.

It is proper to the First Cause to be One—for unity precedes multitude—and to surpass all things in power and goodness. Consequently all things must partake of it. For owing to its power nothing else can hinder it, and owing to its goodness it will not hold itself apart.

If the First Cause were Soul, all things would possess

Soul. If it were Mind, all things would possess Mind. If it were Being, all things would partake of Being. And seeing this quality (i. e. Being) in all things, some men have thought that it was Being. Now if things simply *were*, without being good, this argument would be true, but if things that are *are* because of their goodness, and partake in the good, the First thing must needs be both beyond-Being and good. It is strong evidence of this that noble souls despise Being for the sake of the good, when they face death for their country or friends or for the sake of virtue.—After this inexpressible power come the orders of the Gods.

VI. *On Gods Cosmic and Hypercosmic.*

Of the Gods some are of the world, Cosmic, and some above the world, Hypercosmic. By the Cosmic I mean those who make the Cosmos. Of the Hypercosmic Gods some create Essence, some Mind, and some Soul. Thus they have three orders; all of which may be found in treatises on the subject.

Of the Cosmic Gods some make the World *be*, others animate it, others harmonize it, consisting as it does of different elements; the fourth class keep it when harmonized.

These are four actions, each of which has a beginning, middle, and end, consequently there must be twelve gods governing the world.

Those who make the world are Zeus, Poseidon, and Hephaistos; those who animate it are Demeter, Hera, and Artemis; those who harmonize it are Apollo,

Aphrodite, and Hermes ; those who watch over it are Hestia, Athena, and Ares.

One can see secret suggestions of this in their images. Apollo tunes a lyre ; Athena is armed ; Aphrodite is naked (because harmony creates beauty, and beauty in things seen is not covered).

While these twelve in the primary sense possess the world, we should consider that the other gods are contained in these. Dionysus in Zeus, for instance, Asklepios in Apollo, the Charites in Aphrodite.

We can also discern their various spheres : to Hestia belongs the Earth, to Poseidon water, to Hera air, to Hephaistos fire. And the six superior spheres to the gods to whom they are usually attributed. For Apollo and Artemis are to be taken for the Sun and Moon, the sphere of Kronos should be attributed to Demeter, the ether to Athena, while the heaven is common to all. Thus the orders, powers, and spheres of the Twelve Gods have been explained and celebrated in hymns.

VII. *On the Nature of the World and its Eternity.*

The Cosmos itself must of necessity be indestructible and uncreated. Indestructible because, suppose it destroyed : the only possibility is to make one better than this or worse or the same or a chaos. If worse, the power which out of the better makes the worse must be bad. If better, the maker who did not make the better at first must be imperfect in power. If the same, there will be no use in making it ; if a chaos . . . it is impious even to hear such a thing suggested. These reasons would suffice to show that the World is also uncreated : for if not destroyed, neither is it created. Everything that is created is subject to destruction. And further, since the Cosmos exists by the goodness of God it follows that God must always be good and the world exist. Just as light coexists with the Sun and with fire, and shadow coexists with a body.

Of the bodies in the Cosmos, some imitate Mind and move in orbits ; some imitate Soul and move in a straight line, fire and air upward, earth and water downward. Of those that move in orbits the fixed sphere goes from the east, the Seven from the west. (This is so for various causes, especially lest the creation should be imperfect owing to the rapid circuit of the spheres.[1])

The movement being different, the nature of the bodies must also be different ; hence the celestial body does not burn or freeze what it touches, or do anything else that pertains to the four elements.[2]

And since the Cosmos is a sphere—the zodiac proves that—and in every sphere ' down ' means ' towards the centre ', for the centre is farthest distant from every point, and heavy things fall ' down ' and fall to the earth ⟨it follows that the Earth is in the centre of the Cosmos⟩.

[1] i. e. if the Firmament or Fixed Sphere moved in the same direction as the seven Planets, the speed would become too great. On the circular movement cf. Plot. *Eun.* ii. 2.

[2] The fire of which the heavenly bodies are made is the πέμπτον σῶμα, matter, but different from earthly matter. See p. 170.

All these things are made by the Gods, ordered by Mind, moved by Soul. About the Gods we have spoken already.

VIII. *On Mind and Soul, and that the latter is immortal.*

There is a certain force,[1] less primary than Being but more primary than the Soul, which draws its existence from Being and completes the Soul as the Sun completes the eyes. Of Souls some are rational and immortal, some irrational and mortal. The former are derived from the first Gods, the latter from the secondary.

First, we must consider what soul is. It is, then, that by which the animate differs from the inanimate. The difference lies in motion, sensation, imagination, intelligence. Soul, therefore, when irrational, is the life of sense and imagination; when rational, it is the life which controls sense and imagination and uses reason.

The irrational soul depends on the affections of the body; it feels desire and anger irrationally. The rational soul both, with the help of reason, despises the body, and, fighting against the irrational soul, produces either virtue or vice, according as it is victorious or defeated.

It must be immortal, both because it knows the gods (and nothing mortal knows [2] what is immortal), it

---

[1] Proclus, *Elem. Theol.* xx, calls it ἡ νοερὰ φύσις, *Natura Intellectualis*. There are four degrees of existence : lowest of all, Bodies ; above that, Soul ; above all Souls, this 'Intellectual Nature' ; above that, The One.   [2] i. e. in the full sense of Gnôsis.

looks down upon human affairs as though it stood outside them, and, like an unbodied thing, it is affected in the opposite way to the body. For while the body is young and fine, the soul blunders, but as the body grows old it attains its highest power. Again, every good soul uses mind ; but no body can produce mind : for how should that which is without mind produce mind ? Again, while Soul uses the body as an instrument, it is not in it ; just as the engineer is not in his engines (although many engines move without being touched by any one). And if the Soul is often made to err by the body, that is not surprising. For the arts cannot perform their work when their instruments are spoilt.

IX. *On Providence, Fate, and Fortune.*

This is enough to show the Providence of the Gods. For whence comes the ordering of the world, if there is no ordering power? And whence comes the fact that all things are for a purpose : e. g. irrational soul that there may be sensation, and rational that the earth may be set in order?

But one can deduce the same result from the evidences of Providence in nature : e. g. the eyes have been made transparent with a view to seeing ; the nostrils are above the mouth to distinguish bad-smelling foods ; the front teeth are sharp, to cut food, the back teeth broad to grind it. And we find every part of every object arranged on a similar principle. It is impossible that there should be so much providence in the last details, and none in the first principles. Then the arts of prophecy and of healing, which are part of the Cosmos, come of the good providence of the gods.

All this care for the world, we must believe, is taken by the Gods without any act of will or labour. As bodies which possess some power produce their effects by merely existing : e.g. the sun gives light and heat by merely existing ; so, and far more so, the Providence of the Gods acts without effort to itself and for the good of the objects of its forethought. This solves the problems of the Epicureans, who argue that what is Divine neither has trouble itself nor gives trouble to others.

The incorporeal providence of the Gods, both for bodies and for souls, is of this sort ; but that which is of bodies and in bodies is different from this, and is called Fate, Heimarmenê, because the chain of causes (Heirmos) is more visible in the case of bodies ; and it is for dealing with this Fate that the science of 'Mathematic' has been discovered.[1]

Therefore, to believe that human things, especially their material constitution, are ordered not only by celestial beings but by the Celestial Bodies, is a reasonable and true belief. Reason shows that health and sickness, good fortune and bad fortune, arise according to our deserts from that source. But to attribute men's acts of injustice and lust to Fate, is to make ourselves good and the Gods bad. Unless by chance a man meant by such a statement that in general all things are for the good of the world and for those who are in a natural state, but that bad educa-

---

[1] i. e. Astrology, dealing with the 'Celestial Bodies'.

tion or weakness of nature changes the goods of Fate for the worse. Just as it happens that the Sun, which is good for all, may be injurious to persons with ophthalmia or fever. Else why do the Massagetae eat their fathers, the Hebrews practise circumcision, and the Persians preserve rules of rank? [1] Why do astrologers, while calling Saturn and Mars ' malignant ', proceed to make them good, attributing to them philosophy and royalty, generalships and treasures? And if they are going to talk of triangles and squares, it is absurd that gods should change their natures according to their position in space, while human virtue remains the same everywhere. Also the fact that the stars predict high or low rank for the father of the person whose horoscope is taken, teaches that they do not always make things happen but sometimes only indicate things. For how could things which preceded the birth depend upon the birth?

Further, as there is Providence and Fate concerned with nations and cities, and also concerned with each individual, so there is also Fortune, which should next be treated. That power of the gods which orders for the good things which are not uniform, and which happen contrary to expectation, is commonly called Fortune, and it is for this reason that the goddess is especially worshipped in public by cities; for every city consists of elements which are not uniform. Fortune has power beneath the moon, since above the moon no single thing can happen by fortune.

If Fortune makes a wicked man prosperous and

[1] Cf. Hdt. i. 134.

a good man poor, there is no need to wonder. For the wicked regard wealth as everything, the good as nothing. And the good fortune of the bad cannot take away their badness, while virtue alone will be enough for the good.

X. *Concerning Virtue and Vice.*

The doctrine of Virtue and Vice depends on that of the Soul. When the irrational soul enters into the body and immediately produces Fight and Desire, the rational soul, put in authority over all these, makes the soul tripartite, composed of Reason, Fight, and Desire. Virtue in the region of Reason is Wisdom, in the region of Fight is Courage, in the region of Desire it is Temperance; the virtue of the whole Soul is Righteousness. It is for Reason to judge what is right, for Fight in obedience to Reason to despise things that appear terrible, for Desire to pursue not the apparently desirable, but, that which is with Reason desirable. When these things are so, we have a righteous life; for righteousness in matters of property is but a small part of virtue. And thus we shall find all four virtues in properly trained men, but among the untrained one may be brave and unjust, another temperate and stupid, another prudent and unprincipled. Indeed these qualities should not be called Virtues when they are devoid of Reason and imperfect and found in irrational beings. Vice should be regarded as consisting of the opposite elements. In Reason it is Folly, in Fight, Cowardice, in Desire, Intemperance, in the whole soul, Unrighteousness.

The virtues are produced by the right social organization and by good rearing and education, the vices by the opposite.

XI. *Concerning right and wrong Social Organization.*[1]

Constitutions also depend on the tripartite nature of the Soul. The rulers are analogous to Reason, the soldiers to Fight, the common folk to Desires.

Where all things are done according to Reason and the best man in the nation rules, it is a Kingdom; where more than one rule according to Reason and Fight, it is an Aristocracy; where the government is according to Desire and offices depend on money, that constitution is called a Timocracy. The contraries are: to Kingdom tyranny, for Kingdom does all things with the guidance of reason and tyranny nothing; to Aristocracy oligarchy, when not the best people but a few of the worst are rulers; to Timocracy democracy, when not the rich but the common folk possess the whole power.

XII. *The origin of evil things; and that there is no positive evil.*

The Gods being good and making all things, how do evils exist in the world? Or perhaps it is better first to state the fact that, the Gods being good and making all things, there is no positive evil, it only comes by

[1] [This section is a meagre reminiscence of Plato's discussion in *Repub.* viii. The interest in politics and government had died out with the loss of political freedom.]

absence of good ; just as darkness itself does not exist, but only comes about by absence of light.

If Evil exists it must exist either in Gods or minds or souls or bodies. It does not exist in any god, for all god is good. If any one speaks of a ' bad mind ' he means a mind without mind. If of a bad soul, he will make soul inferior to body, for no body in itself is evil. If he says that Evil is made up of soul and body together, it is absurd that separately they should not be evil, but joined should create evil.

Suppose it is said that there are evil spirits :—if they have their power from the gods, they cannot be evil ; if from elsewhere, the gods do not make all things. If they do not make all things, then either they wish to and cannot, or they can and do not wish ; neither of which is consistent with the idea of God. We may see, therefore, from these arguments, that there is no positive evil in the world.

It is in the activities of men that the evils appear, and that not of all men nor always. And as to these, if men sinned for the sake of evil, Nature itself would be evil. But if the adulterer thinks his adultery bad but his pleasure good, and the murderer thinks the murder bad but the money he gets by it good, and the man who does evil to an enemy thinks that to do evil is bad but to punish his enemy good, and if the soul commits all its sins in that way, then the evils are done for the sake of goodness. (In the same way, because in a given place light does not exist, there comes darkness, which has no positive existence.) The soul sins therefore because, while aiming at good, it makes mistakes about the good, because it is not Primary Essence. And we see many things done by the Gods to prevent it from making mistakes and to heal it when it has made them. Arts and sciences, curses and prayers, sacrifices and initiations, laws and constitutions, judgements and punishments, all came into existence for the sake of preventing souls from sinning ; and when they are gone forth from the body gods and spirits of purification cleanse them of their sins.

XIII. *How things eternal are said to ' be made '* (γίγνεσθαι).

Concerning the Gods and the World and human things this account will suffice for those who are not able to go through the whole course of philosophy but yet have not souls beyond help.

It remains to explain how these objects were never made and are never separated one from another, since we ourselves have said above that the secondary substances were ' made ' by the first.

Everything made is made either by art or by a physical process or according to some power.[1] Now in art or nature the maker must needs be prior to the made : but the maker, according to power, constitutes the made absolutely together with itself, since its power is inseparable from it ; as the sun makes light, fire makes heat, snow makes cold.

Now if the Gods make the world by art, they do

---

[1] κατὰ δύναμιν, secundum potentiam quandam ; i. e. in accordance with some indwelling ' virtue ' or quality.

not make it *be*, they make it *be such as it is*. For all art makes the form of the object. What therefore makes it to be?

If by a physical process, how in that case can the maker help giving part of himself to the made? As the Gods are incorporeal, the World ought to be incorporeal too. If it were argued that the Gods were bodies, then where would the power of incorporeal things come from? And if we were to admit it, it would follow that when the world decays, its maker must be decaying too, if he is a maker by physical process.

If the Gods make the world neither by art nor by physical process, it only remains that they make it by power. Everything so made subsists together with that which possesses the power. Neither can things so made be destroyed, except the power of the maker be taken away : so that those who believe in the destruction of the world, either deny the existence of the gods, or, while admitting it, deny God's power.

Therefore he who makes all things by his own power makes all things subsist together with himself. And since his power is the greatest power he must needs be the maker not only of men and animals, but of Gods, men, and spirits.[1] And the further removed the First God is from our nature, the more powers there must be between us and him. For all things that are very far apart have many intermediate points between them.

---

[1] The repetition of ἀνθρώπους in this sentence seems to be a mistake.

XIV. *In what sense, though the Gods never change, they are said to be made angry and appeased.*

If any one thinks the doctrine of the unchangeableness of the Gods is reasonable and true, and then wonders how it is that they rejoice in the good and reject the bad, are angry with sinners and become propitious when appeased, the answer is as follows : God does not rejoice—for that which rejoices also grieves ; nor is he angered—for to be angered is a passion ; nor is he appeased by gifts—if he were, he would be conquered by pleasure.

It is impious to suppose that the Divine is affected for good or ill by human things. The Gods are always good and always do good and never harm, being always in the same state and like themselves. The truth simply is that, when we are good, we are joined to the Gods by our likeness to them ; when bad, we are separated from them by our unlikeness. And when we live according to virtue we cling to the gods, and when we become evil we make the gods our enemies— not because they are angered against us, but because our sins prevent the light of the gods from shining upon us, and put us in communion with spirits of punishment. And if by prayers and sacrifices we find forgiveness of sins, we do not appease or change the gods, but by what we do and by our turning towards the Divine we heal our own badness and so enjoy again the goodness of the gods. To say that God turns away from the evil is like saying that the sun hides himself from the blind.

XV. *Why we give worship to the Gods when they need nothing.*

This solves the question about sacrifices and other rites performed to the Gods. The Divine itself is without needs, and the worship is paid for our own benefit. The providence of the Gods reaches everywhere and needs only some congruity [1] for its reception. All congruity comes about by representation and likeness; for which reason the temples are made in representation of heaven, the altar of earth, the images of life (that is why they are made like living things), the prayers of the element of thought, the mystic letters [2] of the unspeakable celestial forces, the herbs and stones of matter, and the sacrificial animals of the irrational life in us.

From all these things the Gods gain nothing; what gain could there be to God? It is we who gain some communion with them.

XVI. *Concerning sacrifices and other worships, that we benefit man by them, but not the gods.*

I think it well to add some remarks about sacrifices. In the first place, since we have received everything from the gods, and it is right to pay the giver some tithe of his gifts, we pay such a tithe of possessions in votive offerings, of bodies in gifts of ⟨hair and⟩ adornment, and of life in sacrifices. Then secondly, prayers without sacrifices are only words, with sacri-

---

[1] ἐπιτηδειότης.   [2] On the mystic letters see above, p. 175.

fices they are live words; the word gives meaning to the life, while the life animates the word. Thirdly, the happiness of every object is its own perfection; and perfection for each is communion with its own cause. For this reason we pray for communion with the Gods. Since, therefore, the first life is the life of the gods, but human life is also life of a kind, and human life wishes for communion with divine life, a mean term is needed. For things very far apart cannot have communion without a mean term, and the mean term must be like the things joined; therefore the mean term between life and life must be life. That is why men sacrifice animals; only the rich do so now, but in old days everybody did, and that not indiscriminately, but giving the suitable offerings to each god together with a great deal of other worship. Enough of this subject.

XVII. *That the World is by nature Eternal.*

We have shown above that the gods will not destroy the world. It remains to show that its nature is indestructible.

Everything that is destroyed is either destroyed by itself or by something else. If the world is destroyed by itself, fire must needs burn itself and water dry itself. If by something else, it must be either by a body or by something incorporeal. By something incorporeal is impossible; for incorporeal things preserve bodies—nature, for instance, and soul—and nothing is destroyed by a cause whose nature is to preserve it. If it is destroyed by some body, it must be either by those which exist or by others.

If by those which exist : then either those moving in a straight line must be destroyed by those that revolve, or vice versa. But those that revolve have no destructive nature ; else, why do we never see anything destroyed from that cause? Nor yet can those which are moving straight touch the others ; else, why have they never been able to do so yet?

But neither can those moving straight be destroyed by one another : for the destruction of one is the creation of another ; and that is not to be destroyed but to change.

But if the World is to be destroyed by other bodies than these it is impossible to say where such bodies are or whence they are to arise.

Again, everything destroyed is destroyed either in form or matter. (Form is the shape of a thing, matter the body.) Now if the form is destroyed and the matter remains, we see other things come into being. If matter is destroyed, how is it that the supply has not failed in all these years?

If when matter is destroyed other matter takes its place, the new matter must come either from something that is or from something that is not. If from that-which-is, as long as that-which-is always remains, matter always remains. But if that-which-is is destroyed, such a theory means that not the World only but everything in the universe is destroyed.

If again matter comes from that-which-is-not : in the first place, it is impossible for anything to come from that which is not ; but suppose it to happen, and that matter did arise from that which is not ; then, as long as there are things which are not, matter will exist.   For I presume there can never be an end of things which are not.

If they say that matter ⟨will become⟩ formless :   in the first place, why does this happen to the world as a whole when it does not happen to any part?   Secondly, by this hypothesis they do not destroy the being of bodies, but only their beauty.

Further, everything destroyed is either resolved into the elements from which it came, or else vanishes into not-being.   If things are resolved into the elements from which they came, then there will be others :   else how did they come into being at all?   If that-which-is is to depart into not-being, what prevents that happening to God himself?   (Which is absurd.)   Or if God's power prevents that, it is not a mark of power to be able to save nothing but oneself.   And it is equally impossible for that-which-is to come out of nothing and to depart into nothing.

Again, if the World is destroyed, it must needs either be destroyed according to Nature or against Nature. Against Nature is impossible, for that which is against Nature is not stronger than Nature.[1]   If according to Nature, there must be another Nature which changes the Nature of the World :   which does not appear.

Again, anything that is naturally destructible we can ourselves destroy.   But no one has ever destroyed or altered the round body of the World.   And the

---

[1] The text here is imperfect : I have followed Mullach's correction.

elements, though they can be changed, cannot be destroyed. Again, everything destructible is changed by time and grows old. But the world through all these years has remained utterly unchanged.

Having said so much for the help of those who feel the need of very strong demonstrations, I pray the World himself to be gracious to me.

XVIII. *Why there are rejections of God, and that God is not injured.*

Nor need the fact that rejections of God have taken place in certain parts of the earth and will often take place hereafter, disturb the mind of the wise : both because these things do not affect the gods, just as we saw that worship did not benefit them ; and because the soul, being of middle essence, cannot be always right ; and because the whole world cannot enjoy the providence of the gods equally, but some parts may partake of it eternally, some at certain times, some in the primal manner, some in the secondary. Just as the head enjoys all the senses, but the rest of the body only one.

For this reason, it seems, those who ordained Festivals ordained also Forbidden Days, in which some temples lay idle, some were shut, some had their adornment removed, in expiation of the weakness of our nature.

It is not unlikely, too, that the rejection of God is a kind of punishment : we may well believe that those who knew the gods and neglected them in one life may in another life be deprived of the knowledge of them altogether. Also those who have worshipped their own kings as gods have deserved as their punishment to lose all knowledge of God.

XIX. *Why sinners are not punished at once.*

There is no need to be surprised if neither these sins nor yet others bring immediate punishment upon sinners. For it is not only Spirits [1] who punish the soul, the Soul brings itself to judgement : and also it is not right for those who endure for ever to attain everything in a short time : and also, there is need of human virtue. If punishment followed instantly upon sin, men would act justly from fear and have no virtue.

Souls are punished when they have gone forth from the body, some wandering among us, some going to hot or cold places of the earth, some harassed by Spirits. Under all circumstances they suffer with the irrational part of their nature, with which they also sinned. For its sake [2] there subsists that shadowy body which is seen about graves, especially the graves of evil livers.

XX. *On Transmigration of Souls, and how Souls are said to migrate into brute beasts.*

If the transmigration of a soul takes place into a rational being, it simply becomes the soul of that body. But if the soul migrates into a brute beast, it follows

---

[1] δαίμονες.
[2] i. e. that it may continue to exist and satisfy justice.

the body outside, as a guardian spirit follows a man.
For there could never be a rational soul in an irrational
being.

The transmigration of souls can be proved from the
congenital afflictions of persons. For why are some
born blind, others paralytic, others with some sickness
in the soul itself? Again, it is the natural duty of Souls
to do their work in the body ; are we to suppose that
when once they leave the body they spend all eternity
in idleness?

Again, if the souls did not again enter into bodies,
they must either be infinite in number or God must
constantly be making new ones. But there is nothing
infinite in the world ; for in a finite whole there cannot
be an infinite part. Neither can others be made ; for
everything in which something new goes on being
created, must be imperfect. And the World, being
made by a perfect author, ought naturally to be perfect.

XXI. *That the Good are happy, both living and dead.*

Souls that have lived in virtue are in general happy,[1]
and when separated from the irrational part of their
nature, and made clean from all matter, have communion with the gods and join them in the governing
of the whole world. Yet even if none of this happiness
fell to their lot, virtue itself, and the joy and glory of
virtue, and the life that is subject to no grief and no
master are enough to make happy those who have set
themselves to live according to virtue and have
achieved it.

[1] εὐδαιμονοῦσι.

INDEX